# Investing in Oil and Gas

Mike May, P.E.

www. Investing in Oil and Gas .com

# Geologic Time Scale

| Eon | Era | Period | | Epoch | Million Years Ago |
|---|---|---|---|---|---|
| Phanerozoic | Cenozoic | Quaternary | | HOLOCENE | 0.0117 |
| | | | | Pleistocene | 2.6 |
| | | Tertiary | Neogene | Pliocene | 5 |
| | | | | Miocene | 23 |
| | | | Paleogene | Oligocene | 34 |
| | | | | Eocene | 56 |
| | | | | Paleocene | 65.5 |
| | Mesozoic | Cretaceous | | | 146 |
| | | Jurassic | | | 200 |
| | | Triassic | | | 251 |
| | Paleozoic | Permian | | | 299 |
| | | Pennsylvanian | | | 318 |
| | | Mississippian | | | 359 |
| | | Devonian | | | 416 |
| | | Silurian | | | 444 |
| | | Ordovician | | | 488 |
| | | Cambrian | | | 542 |

In the interest of full disclosure, the author owns an oil and gas exploration and production company, invests in oil and gas, and provides technical consulting services.

Investing in Oil and Gas
Second Edition


Mike May, P.E.
(832) 382-9976
mike.may @ investing in oil and gas .com
www. investing in oil and gas .com

Investors Publishing
www.investorspublishing.com

*ISBN-13: 978-0615434575 (Investors Publishing)*

This book is dedicated
to my mother and father.

## Acknowledgements:

I would like to acknowledge all of the skills, knowledge, experience, and strenuous effort put forth by the people in the oilfield service industry.

You are the oilfield.

# Contents

## Chapter 2: Geology (Continued)

## Chapter 3: Finding a Prospect 75



## Chapter 4: Drilling a Well 85

## Chapter 5: Formation Evaluation 123



## Chapter 6: Completion 153

# Part II: Oil and Gas Business

## Part III: 150 Questions to Consider Before You Invest

# Introduction

What if I buried $5 million dollars in a treasure chest just 25 feet underground and then I told you that you can have the chest and everything inside if you can just get it out of the ground?

Do you think you would find a way to get it out? Of course! You might dig it out with a shovel. You might get excavating equipment. You might dig a tunnel from the side. But one way or another you would find a way to dig it out. Unfortunately I can't make that offer.

But what if someone buried several million dollars a few thousand feet underground? And what if they repeated this act in not just one place but in hundreds of locations around the country and I told you that you can have it all if you can just find it and get it out? That is surprisingly real and the offer stands!

Millions of barrels of oil and billions of cubic feet of natural gas are indeed buried just a few thousand feet below our toes in countless locations throughout the country. Think about it for a minute.

There are tens and even hundreds of millions of dollars waiting for us just a few thousand of feet underground. All we have to do is get it out.

I can't think of a more rewarding or more thrilling pursuit in life!

You don't pick up an oil and gas investing book if you want to earn 1% to 5% returns on your money. There are plenty of simpler and safer ways to obtain those returns. You pick up an oil and gas book when you want to earn multiples of your initial investment. This is how fortunes are made and multiplied.

Super-normal profits are possible by drilling wells because the magnitude of your return is not proportional to the size of your investment. Your investment is dependent on the cost of creating a well. But your returns are determined by the breadth and thickness of the oil and gas reservoirs that your well penetrates.

The right to drill in to reservoirs containing millions of dollars can be obtained with one simple document – an oil and gas lease. And you can acquire a lease in the United States for as little as a few thousand dollars.

If you are interested in joining small groups of private investors who drill their own oil and natural gas wells in the United States then this book is for you. I hope you will find it to be informative. I have divided this book in to three parts that I think are important.

The first part provides a description of the fundamentals of oil and gas operations. It covers petroleum chemistry, geology, seismic surveying, drilling a well, formation evaluation, completions, production, reservoir drive mechanisms, selling your oil and natural gas, workovers, and finally plugging and abandoning a well.

The second part delves deeply into the business side of your investments. We will discuss oil and gas leases, oil and gas law, deal structures, economic evaluation of investment opportunities, and federal taxation.

The third part of this book provides you with over 150 specific questions to consider before you invest in any particular oil and gas deal. Considering these questions will push your understanding of any investment you are contemplating to a deeper level and serve as a resource when you are performing due diligence.

I wrote this book to help people who are interested in drilling oil and natural gas wells in the United States. I wanted to share my knowledge so that you might benefit in money and in meaning.

I look forward to hearing from you. And I wish you the best of luck in your drilling ventures!

Mike May, P.E.
(832) 382-9976
mike.may@investing in oil and gas .com
www. investing in oil and gas .com
www. limestone oil .com

# Chapter 1
# Petroleum

What is Petroleum? Petroleum is a complex mixture of hydrocarbons. Hydrocarbons are molecules that are composed of the elements of hydrogen (H) and carbon (C). In nature, hydrogen and carbon combine in an infinite number of ways to create an infinite number of hydrocarbon molecules. Carbon has a valence of four and hydrogen has a valence of one. So hydrocarbon molecules tend to form structures that satisfy these valence numbers. The simplest hydrocarbon molecule is methane. It contains a single carbon atom and four hydrogen atoms. Oil and natural gas are the liquid and gaseous phases of petroleum.

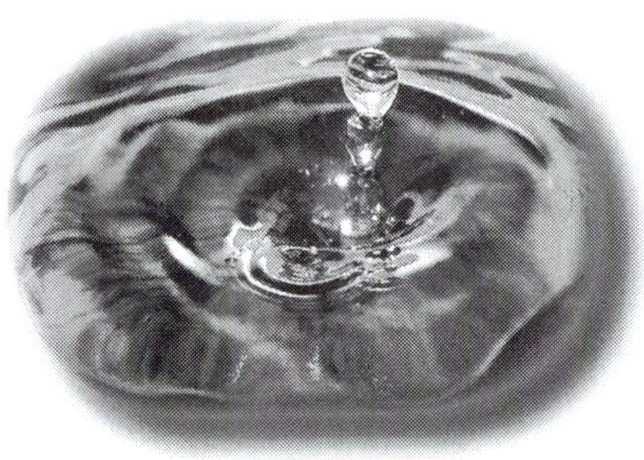

## Hydrocarbon Groups

There are three major groups of hydrocarbons: alkanes, naphthenes, and aromatics.

## Alkanes

The chemical formula of the first group of hydrocarbons, called alkanes, is $C_nH_{2n+2}$ where n represents a varying number of carbon atoms in the

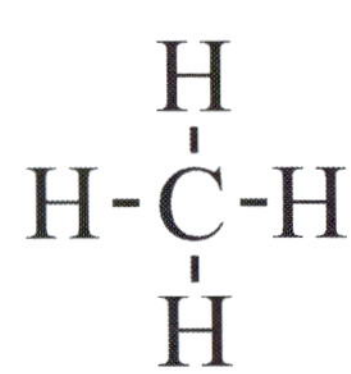

Methane

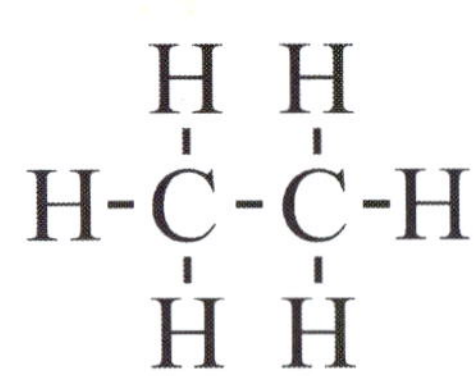

Ethane

molecules. Alkanes are chains of carbon atoms surrounded by hydrogen atoms. Common hydrocarbons that are of interest in the petroleum industry are the first eight members of the alkanes group: methane ($CH_4$), ethane ($C_2H_6$), propane ($C_3H_8$), butane ($C_4H_{10}$), pentane ($C_5H_{12}$), hexane ($C_6H_{14}$), heptane ($C_7H_{16}$), and octane ($C_8H_{18}$).

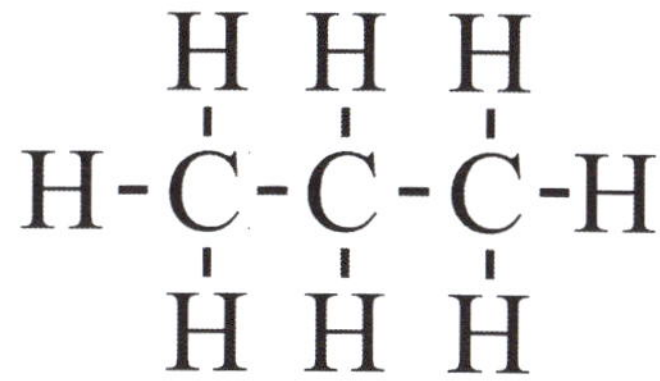

Propane

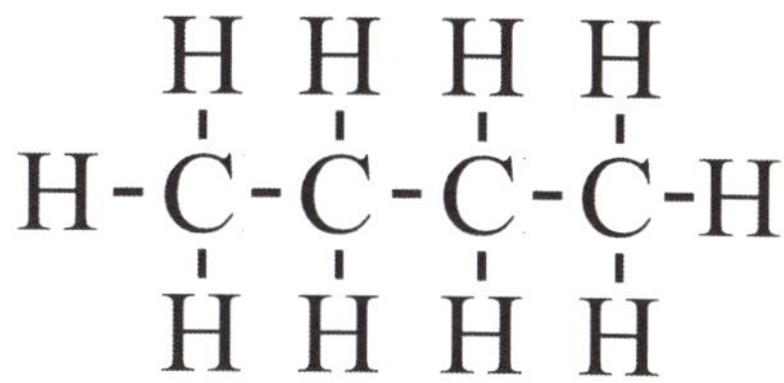

Butane

Alkane molecules with more than 20 carbon atoms are waxy solids at surface temperature and pressure. They are called paraffins.

# Naphthenes

Hydrocarbon molecules also form in rings with the chemical formula of $C_nH_{2n}$. These are called naphthenes.

# Aromatic Hydrocarbons

Benzene is a ring-shaped molecule that has the chemical formula of $C_6H_6$. To meet the valence requirements, a benzene ring includes three single bonds and three double bonds between the carbon atoms. The benzene ring is the foundation of the group of hydrocarbons called aromatic hydrocarbons.

# Liquids and Gases

Crude oil contains thousands of different kinds of alkanes, naphthenes, and aromatic hydrocarbons.
The term "petroleum" includes liquid crude oil, natural gas, and mixtures

of the two. Some molecules can be dissolved in liquid crude oil at the higher pressures and temperatures that exist in a subsurface reservoir; but they will bubble out of solution and assume a gaseous phase when the crude oil is brought to the surface where pressures and temperatures are lower. You have probably observed a similar phenomenon when you have opened the cap on a bottle of soda. As you released the internal pressure, carbon dioxide molecules changed from a liquid phase to a gas phase and then bubbled up to the top of the bottle. A similar event occurs in some oil reservoirs when the reservoir pressure falls below the bubble point pressure.

Natural gas reservoirs can also hold certain hydrocarbon molecules such as propane and butane in a gaseous phase while they are at downhole pressures and temperatures; but they will precipitate out of the gas and assume a liquid phase when they are brought from the higher pressures and temperatures downhole to the lower pressures and temperatures at the surface. These molecules are commonly called condensates or distillates. The gas that contains these kinds of molecules is called a condensate gas because it contains some molecules that will condense in to liquid phase when the pressure and temperature are reduced.

Depending on its molecular composition, petroleum may be 100% liquid, 100% gas, or part liquid and part gas at any given combination of pressure and temperature. A representative sample of petroleum from a reservoir can be tested in a laboratory to establish its phase behavior at any combination of pressure and temperature.

# Crude Oil

Crude oil composition varies. So its energy content, color, density, viscosity, and commercial value also vary. Crude oil can be clear, green, brown, yellowish, black, and all shades of color in between. The density varies from roughly half of the density of water to denser than water. It can flow easily or resist flow much like honey. Its viscosity varies with temperature. Other compounds such as $CO_2$, $H_2S$, along with Oxygen, Nitrogen, and saline water are sometimes found in petroleum in small amounts.

## Hydrogen Sulfide

Hydrogen sulfide ($H_2S$) is a poisonous gas. Petroleum that contains hydrogen sulfide ($H_2S$) is called "sour crude" or "sour gas". "Sweet crude" refers to crude that does not contain hydrogen sulfide. Special precautions must be taken in the drilling, production, and transportation of sour crude and sour gas. In addition to being more costly to produce, hydrogen sulfide ($H_2S$) diminishes the value of petroleum because it increases the cost of transporting and refining it. It can also hasten the corrosion of metal equipment in the wellbore and in surface facilities that comes in contact with it. Fortunately, hydrogen sulfide is not a concern in the majority of wells.

## Natural Gas

Natural Gas is a mixture of hydrocarbons that occur naturally in underground reservoirs in a gaseous phase. Natural gas composition is usually limited to varying amounts of methane ($CH_4$), ethane ($C_2H_6$), propane ($C_3H_8$), butane ($C_4H_{10}$), carbon dioxide ($CO_2$), oxygen ($O_2$), nitrogen ($N_2$), and hydrogen sulfide ($H_2S$). But not all natural gases contain all of these molecules. Natural gas may also contain trace amounts of Helium, Neon, and Xenon. The term "dry gas" refers to a natural gas mixture that is almost entirely methane. It will exist in a gaseous phase under almost every combination of pressure and temperature. The word "dry" refers to the fact that no liquids will precipitate out of it at lower pressures and temperatures. A "wet gas" is a natural gas mixture that contains 80% to 90% methane with the remainder of the molecules including the natural gas liquids of ethane ($C_2H_6$), propane ($C_3H_8$), butane ($C_4H_{10}$) and some larger alkanes. Some of these molecules will precipitate out of the gas in to a liquid state at surface pressure and temperature. Hence the name "wet gas". Wet gas is also called condensate gas.

## Looking Ahead

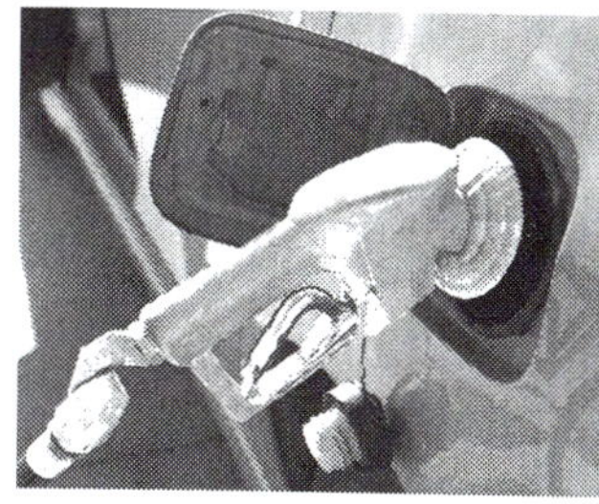

Oil and natural gas provide well over 50% of the energy consumed in the United States.

According to the U.S. government's Energy Information Administration, the dominance of oil and natural gas as America's fuel will continue through the next 25 years and beyond.

For more, visit www.eia.doe.gov

# Chapter 2
# Geology

Geology is the study of the Earth. And some knowledge of geology is necessary when one is exploring for oil and gas. Geology is composed of two broad areas: physical geology and historical geology.

Physical geology pertains to the processes both above and below the Earth's surface that create and change the physical parts of the Earth – especially rock formations. This includes the continents, oceans, volcanoes, mountain building, sedimentation, erosion, faulting, fracturing, and folding, and the formation of minerals, ores, and oil and natural gas.

Historical geology pertains to the history of the Earth and the events that have shaped the Earth on a macroscopic scale throughout its past. It answers questions like when the Earth was formed, when life began to appear, when life began to flourish, what kinds of life forms lived during what time periods, when a region was covered by shallow seas, when it was dry land, when it was uplifted, when it was down warped, what geographic features existed in what places during what time periods, when continents collided to form mountains, when continents pulled apart, when rock layers were deposited and when they were eroded, when basins were filled with sediment, and so on.

In a sense, physical geology explains how things happened and historical geology explains when things happened. Together physical and historical geology explain how and when things happened and why they are the way they are today.

Let's step back in time for a short review of the history of the Earth, the creation of the continents, the history of life on Earth, and the creation of sedimentary rocks. Once we understand how rocks were formed we will have a much better idea of how and where petroleum was created and where to look for it.

## Plate Tectonics

Present day geologic thinking is driven by the theory of plate tectonics. This theory only reached wide acceptance as recently as the 1960's. Plate tectonics explains the geologic features we see at the Earth's surface and far below.

The story goes like this. At the center of the Earth is a solid spherical core made

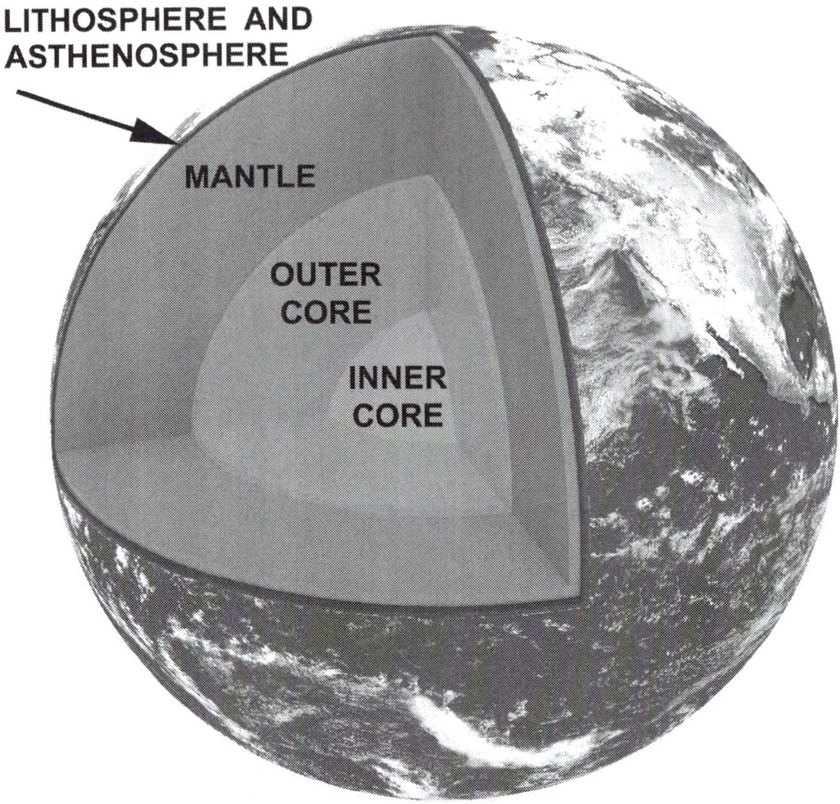


of iron-nickel metal that is approximately 2400 km in diameter. Surrounding the solid inner core is a liquid outer core also composed of iron and nickel that is approximately 2300 km thick. The next layer is the mantle. It is a viscous material that is about 2900 km thick. Continuing outward, there is a thin layer called the asthenosphere which is composed of molten flowing rock that is about 200 km thick. Moving outward again, the next layer is the lithosphere which is composed of rigid rock. It is roughly 80 km thick. At the outer part of the lithosphere is a thin crust. The crust is 5 to 75 km thick and we reside on its outer surface. There are two kinds of crust: continental crust and oceanic crust.

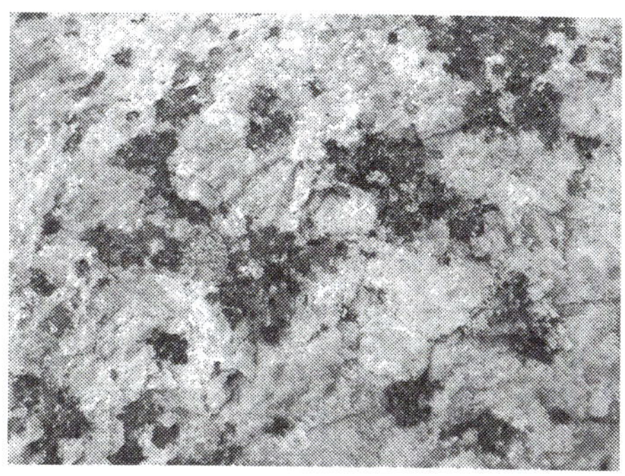

**Granite**

Continental crust is composed predominantly of granite. Granite is an igneous rock that contains varying amounts of potassium feldspar, plagioclase feldspar, amphibole, biotite, and quartz.

Oceanic crust is composed primarily of a denser material known as basalt. Basalt is an igneous rock that is produced where magma is extruded on the ocean floor. Basalt is composed primarily of plagioclase feldspar and pyroxene.

The Earth's lithosphere which includes the crust is broken in to sheets or plates which float on the deeper molten asthenosphere. Generally the oceanic plates are heavier than the continental plates because they are composed of basalt while the continental plates are composed of the less dense and lighter granite.

## Convection Causes the Plates to Move

As heat from natural radioactive decay occurring in the Earth's core is transferred outward by conduction, the inner most portions of the liquid mantle and asthenosphere become hotter and less dense than the material above them. So they become buoyant in a relative sense and they move outward. Simultaneously cooler denser material is less buoyant and moves inward toward the core. This is similar to the convection currents one can observe in a pot of boiling water. Convection currents below the Earth's surface pull on the plates that are floating on the surface and cause them to move just like floating objects in a pot of boiling water.

This diagram is from the U.S. Geological Survey. It shows the positions of continental plates as they have floated around on Earth's asthenosphere since the breakup of Pangea began during the Triassic Period.

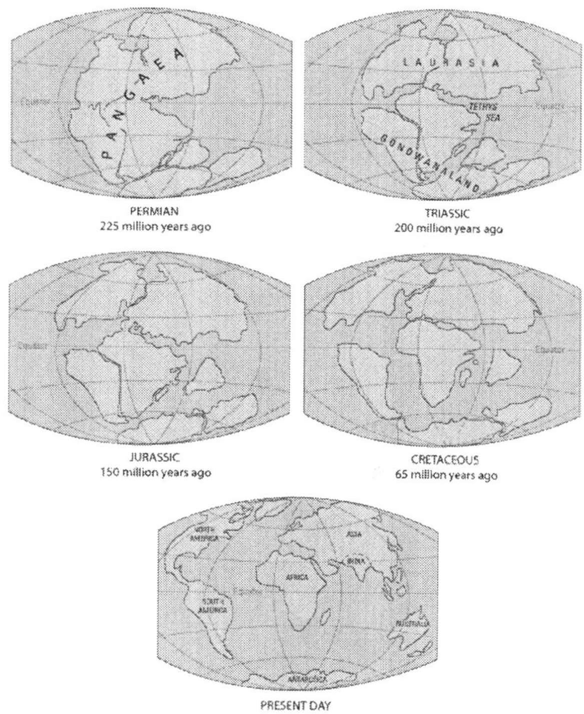


**Source: US Geological Survey**

When two plates collide, mountains can be pushed up and one of the plates can be subducted below the other plate. The Himalayan Mountains were formed as the Indian plate collided with and was subducted below the Eurasian plate. The crumpling effect pushed up the Himalayas.

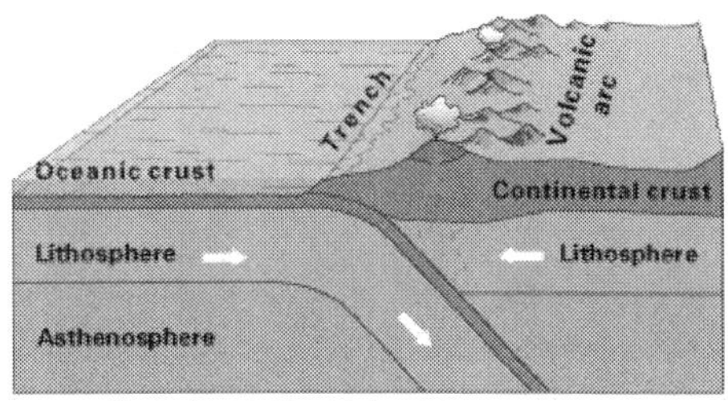

Oceanic-continental convergence

**Convergence of Plates**
**Source: USGS**

If one plate slides beneath another plate, the subducted plate can be melted and the resulting lava can be pushed up through cracks in the overlying plate to produce volcanoes. The volcanoes in the Andes Mountain range are examples of this process as the Nazca plate and the Antarctic plates are converging with and being subducted below the South American plate.

When plates spread apart, a gap or rift develops and molten rock from below can push up through the opening. The Mid-Atlantic ridge is an example of a boundary where plates are spreading apart. The North American and South American plates are moving away from the Eurasian and African plates.

If plates move apart but molten rock from below does not pierce the surface then a depression in the Earth's crust may form a basin where other sediments accumulate. The Gulf of Mexico is an example of this.

## Folds

**Folded Rock Formations**

During tectonic convergence, rock layers are subjected to compressive stress. As a result they bend or crack or both bend and crack. The bending of rock formations is called folding. Folding creates underground structures. Synclines are U-shaped or bowl-shaped structures that result from folding. Anticlines are upside down U-shaped or upside down bowl-shaped formations that can trap and hold oil and gas. There are numerous places around the world where rocks with these folded structures have been eroded near the surface and we are able to observe them.

## Faults

**A fault between sandstones**

Sedimentary formations can also respond to tectonic compressive stress by fracturing. When fractures form, massive blocks of rock on either side of the fracture can move along the plane of the fracture. These are called faults.

Faults are fractures or cracks through rock where the rock on one side of the fracture has moved relative to the rock on the other side of the fracture. When a fault occurs, the blocks on either side of the fault plane can move up, down, or sideways relative to the rocks on the other side of the fault plane. In the oil industry, the term fracture is usually reserved to describe a crack in a rock formation where there has been no relative movement of the rocks on either side of the crack.

## Reverse Fault

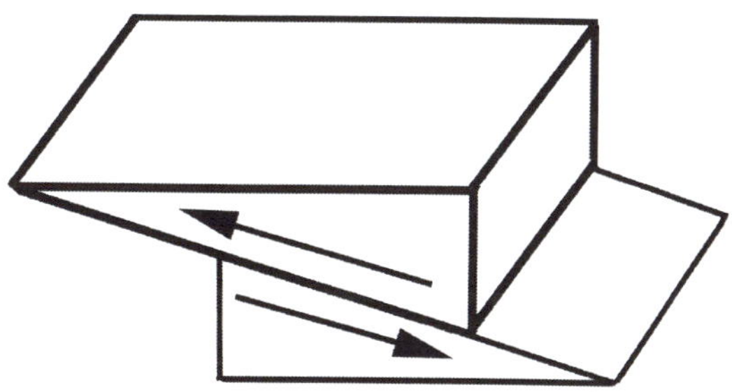

**Reverse Fault**

When a fault forms and the rock layers above the fault plane (called the hanging wall) are pushed up and over the rock layers below the fault plane (called the foot wall) the fault is known as a reverse fault. The side of the fault where the rock has moved up relative to the other side is called the up-thrown side. The side of the fault where the rock has moved down relative to the other side is called the down-thrown side.

## Normal Fault

During tectonic extension or separation, rock layers are subjected to tensile stress.

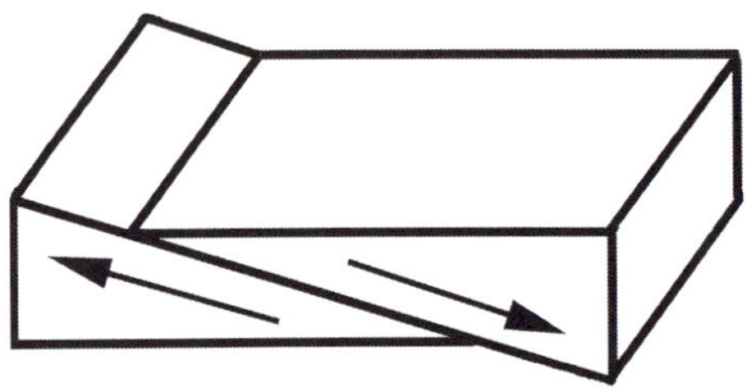

Normal Fault

**Example of a Normal Fault**

Under tensile stress faults may form as blocks of rock are being pulled apart. Some blocks of rock will slide down a fault plane as they move away from the rock on the other side of the fault. These are called normal faults. The side of the fault where the rock layers have moved down relative to the other side is called the down-thrown side of the normal fault. The other side is called the up-thrown side.

## Fault Trap

A fault plane can provide a sealing surface that can trap oil and gas in a permeable formation on one side of the fault against the impermeable formation on the other side of the fault. This kind of trap is called a fault trap.

**Fault Trap**

# The Origin of Petroleum

**A fossil of a plant from the Pennsylvanian Period**

It is widely believed that petroleum formed when organic matter from ancient plants and animals was deposited and subsequently buried under thousands of feet of sedimentary rock over millions of years. As a result of being buried under thousands of feet of sediments, the organic matter was heated and compressed and much of the organic matter was converted to hydrocarbons.

# Source Rock

A layer of sedimentary rock that contains the original organic matter that was converted to petroleum is known as Source Rock. It is usually a bed of shale. The theory that oil and gas were created from organic matter is only a theory. No one knows with certainty.

**Shale**

Oil and natural gas are found in reservoirs as shallow as a few hundred feet to as deep as 15,000 feet below the Earth's surface. Higher temperatures and pressures break down hydrocarbon molecules in to smaller and smaller sizes. At depths below 15,000 feet, hydrocarbons are almost always in the gaseous phase only and are almost entirely composed of methane ($CH_4$).

# Petroleum in the Pores of Sedimentary Rocks

Many people imagine that oil and natural gas accumulate in large underground pools or lakes. But they actually accumulate in underground layers of sedimentary rock in the tiny pore spaces between individual grains of rock.

**Pore Space Model: The steel balls represent individual grains of rock. The spaces between the balls represent the pores where oil and gas accumulate.**

# Upward Migration

Most pore spaces in underground sedimentary rock formations are filled with saline water called formation water or connate water. When hydrocarbons are formed they enter the pore space and share that pore space with the formation water. Being lighter and less dense than water, oil and natural gas are buoyant in water. So they tend to slowly migrate up toward the surface.

If there are no obstructions the oil or gas will continue to move up through the water-filled pores of shallower and shallower formations until it reaches the surface. When oil or gas reaches the surface it is called a natural seepage. The presence of seepages in an area is an indication that there may be more oil and gas below the surface.

# Traps

However, if the oil or gas encounters and impenetrable layer of rock during its journey toward the surface, it will become trapped under that layer of rock. As additional molecules of oil and gas migrate up through the subsurface rock layers and encounter the same impenetrable layer, they too will become trapped and thus a larger and larger amount of petroleum will accumulate in the porous and permeable layer that is immediately below the impenetrable layer. Such an accumulation is known as a reservoir and the seal above the reservoir that will not allow it to migrate up any further is known as a trap. There are several different kinds of traps: anticline traps, fault traps, unconformity traps, and stratigraphic traps.

# Anticline Trap

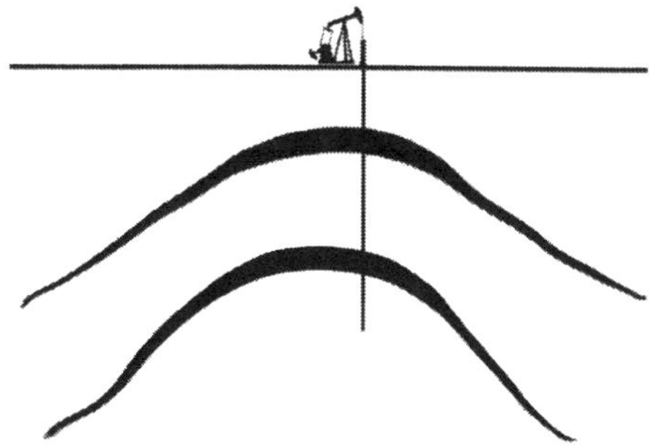

Anticline Traps

In an anticline trap, oil and gas has accumulated in the highest part of a layer of rock that is folded. The classic example is an underground dome shaped layer of rock with oil and or gas accumulated in the top of the dome.

**An anticline exposed on the surface. The grey line marks a fault plane.**

# Fault Trap

In a fault trap oil and gas accumulates in a layer of sedimentary rock that terminates against an impermeable rock formation along a fault plane.

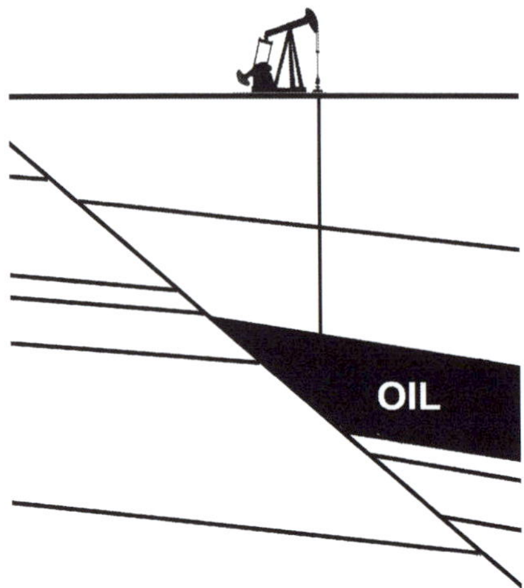


**Fault Trap**

# Stratigraphic Trap

In a stratigraphic trap, oil and gas accumulates in a layer of sedimentary rock that terminates at the limits of the rock layer's lateral extent at the time of its deposition.

**Stratigraphic Trap**

# Unconformity Trap

In an unconformity trap oil and gas accumulate in a layer of sedimentary rock that terminates against an impermeable rock formation where a geologic unconformity exists.

An unconformity is a surface where sediment deposition is not continuous with time so a portion of the geologic record is missing. It can be an ancient eroded surface upon which younger sediments have been deposited.

**Unconformity Trap**

The material that was eroded is missing and thus there is an unconformity.

# Physical Geology

## Minerals in the Earth's Crust

Rocks are mixtures of minerals. Minerals are compounds in the Earth's crust that are composed of certain elements. Surprisingly, there are just twelve elements that make up over 99% of the mass of the Earth's crust. They are oxygen, silicon, aluminum, calcium, magnesium, sodium, potassium, titanium, hydrogen, manganese, and phosphorus. Silicon and oxygen make up over 70% of the mass of the Earth's crust by themselves. As a result of there being a limited number of common elements in the crust, there are consequently a limited number of common minerals in the crust. And as a result most rocks are fabricated from a limited number of minerals.

The bonds within the $(SiO_4)^{-4}$ anion are very strong. This tetrahedral shaped anion bonds with many different cations to form a group of minerals called silicates. There are about 25 common silicates in the Earth's crust. Minerals that contain the $O^{2-}$ anion are called oxides. Silicate minerals, a small number of oxides, and calcium carbonate ($CaCO_3$) together make up about 99% of the Earth's crust. And they are the most common mineral components of the rocks we study in geology.

## Rocks

Rocks are mixtures of minerals. They are almost always in solid phase at atmospheric pressure and temperature and remain in solid phase at much higher pressures and temperatures within the Earth's crust. There are three classes of rocks: igneous, sedimentary, and metamorphic.

## Igneous Rocks

Igneous rocks are formed by magmas rising up from far below the Earth's surface and then cooling and hardening at or near the Earth's surface. At present, very few igneous rocks are known to hold reservoirs of oil or gas. There are a small number of instances where gas has been found within the fractures of igneous rocks.

## Metamorphic Rocks

Metamorphic rocks are formed by altering the form and mineralogy of previously existing rocks with immense heat and or pressure.
Very few metamorphic rocks are known to hold reservoirs of oil or gas.

# Sedimentary Rocks

Sedimentary rocks can be divided in to three types: Carbonates, Clastics, and Precipitates. Most of the oil and gas in the world has been produced from clastics and carbonates. Sedimentary rocks may contain a wide array of minerals but the most common minerals are quartz, feldspar, clays, calcite, dolomite, and evaporites.

## Carbonates

**A modern day reef. The white material on the left is small grains of recent calcium carbonate sediment.**

Carbonates are composed primarily of limestone which is the mineral calcite ($Ca\ CO_3$). In some cases magnesium enters the calcite and replaces half of the calcium and changes the calcite

**A modern example of a broad shallow sea where calcium carbonate sediments are being deposited. Sediments accumulate and may lithify millions of years later to form limestone. Shallow seas such as this covered most of Texas and much of North America throughout most of the Paleozoic era and again during the later Cretaceous period.**

to dolomite ($CaMg(CO_3)_2$).

Carbonate sedimentary rocks were formed in ancient seas from the deposition of the remains of marine organisms that contained calcite in their bodies and from calcite excreted by living organisms as a result of their natural bodily processes. Such organisms include algae, shells, and single-cell organisms. Examples of marine life from the Paleozoic

**Interstate 10 passes through limestone formations in Texas that were deposited in shallow marine seas during the Cretaceous period. These sedimentary formations do not end at the road surface. They continue down for thousands of feet underground.**

period whose skeletons were composed of calcite include mollusks, arthropods, brachiopods, bivalves, echinoderms, sponges, bryozoans, cephalopods, gastropods, algae, and anthozoans.

Carbonate depositional environments include both shallow marine environments such as coral reefs and deep sea floor environments known as benthic environments. The sediments accumulate on the sea floor and build up over time. After millions of years they lithify and become limestone rock formations. If magnesium later replaces half of the calcium then the mineral changes from calcite to dolomite.

Chalk formations are carbonate formations that were deposited in benthic (deep sea floor) environments. Perhaps 60% of all known oil and gas reservoirs in the world are carbonates.

# Clastics

Clastic rocks are formed when older rocks are broken down by weathering or biogenic processes, then transported by water, wind, or ice, and finally deposited in layers of sediment. Most but not all layers of sedimentary rock are deposited in flat horizontal layers. These layers of sediment are later compacted by the weight of later sediments deposited above them. They harden (lithify) to form continuous solid rock. Clastic rocks are classified by their grain size. From largest to smallest grain size they are classified as conglomerates, sandstone, siltstone, mudstone, or shale. Shale has the smallest grain sizes. Shale is a general description for a rock that is usually deposited in a low-energy environment and is composed of varying amounts of hydrous aluminosilicate clays such as kaolinite, illite, and smectite, together with fine-grain silica (silts), calcite, and sometimes organic material known as kerogen. Shales are often found interbedded or mixed with sandstone. Clean sandstone is a term that means sandstone without shale. Sandstone that contains a lot of shale is called a shaley sand. Perhaps 40% of all known oil and gas reservoirs in the world are clastics.

## Precipitates

Precipitate sedimentary rocks form when material precipitates from an aqueous solution and later lithifys to form a solid layer of a nearly pure mineral. The most common examples are evaporates such as salt (NaCl) and gypsum ($CaSO_4 \cdot 2H_2O$) which can form in vast thick layers when the water in an isolated sea evaporates.

# Geologic Time Scale

One of the greatest stories on Earth is the story of Earth itself. The Earth is approximately 4.5 billion years old. Geologists have divided that time in to smaller blocks of time and given those blocks of time names for ease of communication. They call the list of names the Geologic Time Scale. The largest blocks of time are called Eons. Eons are divided in to Eras. Eras are further divided into Periods. Periods are divided in to Epochs. Epochs are divided into Ages. The diagram to the right shows the Geologic Time Scale for the most recent 542 million years of Earth's history which is known as the Phanerozoic Eon. This eon is of the most interest to Petroleum Geologists because most life on Earth has lived during this time and it is in rocks of this eon where most organic matter exists and where most oil and gas reservoirs are found.

# Geologic Time Scale

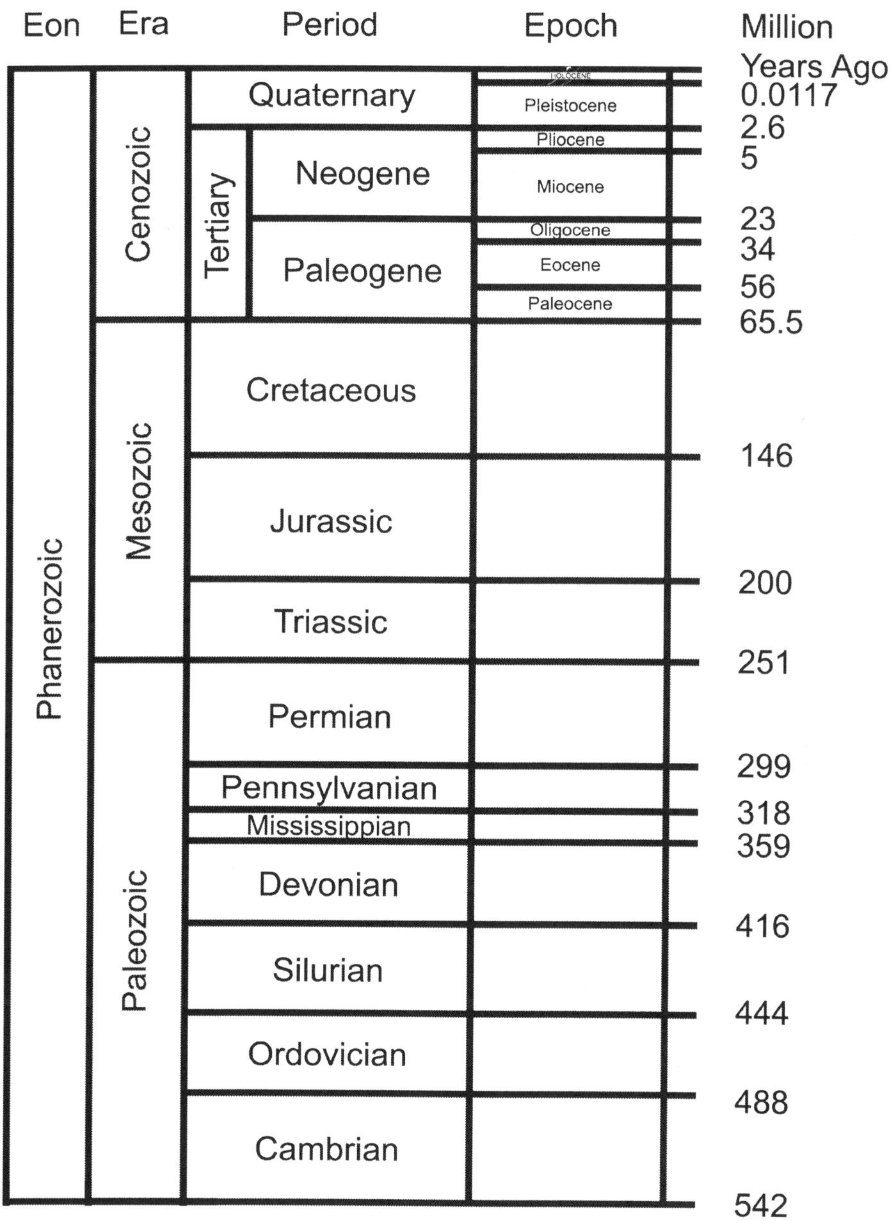

Many sedimentary rocks contain fossils of plants and animals that only lived during the time the sediments were deposited. The fossils include bones, skeletons, leaves, branches, and even foot prints. During the 1800's Geologists observed that certain plants and animals were prevalent at certain times in Earth's history. There was a uniform chronologic order of appearances and extinctions for numerous plant and animal species worldwide. So plants and animals of a particular species were only found in a particular group of rocks that were deposited during a particular time in Earth's history – regardless of where on Earth a fossil was found. It was this chronologic ordering of the existence of certain species that lead to the creation of the geologic periods in the geologic time scale. Certain species were prevalent in certain layers of rock so a geologic period was defined for rocks of that age.

Although they had determined the sequence in which rock formations were deposited, scientists in the 1800's did not know the precise age of the formations deposited during each geologic period. They only knew the sequence of the periods. They knew that Paleozoic rocks were older than Mesozoic rocks but they didn't know exactly how old they were. It was not until the early 20$^{th}$ century that radioactive dating was used to determine the age of rocks. People were shocked to learn that the rocks they were studying were not a few thousand years old as they had guessed but hundreds of millions of years old. And the Earth itself was not a few million years old, but closer to 4,500 million years old.
That's 4.5 Billion years old!

For more information about the geologic time scale, visit

www.geosociety.org/science/timescale/

# Earth's History

## Archean Eon

During the Archean Eon (4.5 - 2.5 billion years ago), the Earth cooled from a molten mass in the newly formed solar system to a planet similar to what we have today with a core at the center of the Earth, a mantle between the core and the surface, and a thin crust at the surface. By the end of the Archean Eon 2.5 billion years ago, there were continents, oceans, and an oxygen-rich atmosphere. The continental plates were composed of large expanses of granite while the oceanic plates were composed of denser basaltic crust just as they are today. The only evidence of life forms that existed during that time is of single-cell cyano bacteria (also called blue-green algae) that created underwater structures called stromatolites. Stromatolites are layered accumulations of calcium carbonate excreted by bacteria. Stromatolites can be centimeters to meters in diameter. Stromatolites constructed by present-day living bacteria can still be found in today's oceans.

## Proterozoic Eon

The next segment of Earth's history was from 2.5 billion years ago to just 542 million years ago. It is called the Proterozoic Eon. During that time the oceans became oxygenated and by the end of the Proterozoic Eon, the basic pieces were in place for a flurry of life on Earth that has taken place between 542 million years ago and today.

## Pre-Cambrian Time

The first 4,000 million years of the Earth's history, which includes the Archean and Proterozoic Eons, is often called Pre-Cambrian time because it all preceded the Cambrian period. The Cambrian period began 542 million years ago. It was the first period of the Phanerozoic Eon which extended from that time to the present.

At the end of Pre-Cambrian time the continents consisted almost entirely of barren granite with very few life forms. There was very little life on Earth. Only very small organisms such as algae have been found in rocks created during this time.

## Phanerozoic Eon

Then about 542 million years ago, in one of the greatest spectacles the Earth has ever seen, and for reasons we cannot easily explain, life suddenly burst upon the scene in abundance. It was the Cambrian period, which occured between 542 and 488 million years ago, there were more species of plants and animals on Earth than at any time since then. It was called the "Cambrian Explosion". This explosion of life marked the end of the 4,000 million year long Pre-Cambrian time and the beginning of the Phanerozoic Eon.

The Phanerozoic Eon is divided into three eras: the Paleozoic era, the Mesozoic era, and the Cenozoic era.

The Paleozoic era began 542 million years ago and ended 245 million years ago. During the Paleozoic era, life developed from marine invertebrates to fish and amphibians and finally reptiles.

The Mesozoic era began 245 million years ago and ended 65 million years ago. It was dominated by dinosaurs.

The Cenozoic era began 65 million years ago and extends to the present day. Mammals have dominated the Cenozoic era.

Each of these three eras is further divided in to smaller geologic periods. The Paleozoic era is divided into the Cambrian, Ordovician, Silurian, Devonian, Mississippian, Pennsylvanian, and Permian periods. The Mesozoic era is divided in to the Triassic, Jurassic, and Cretaceous periods. And finally the Cenozoic era is divided in to the Tertiary and Quaternary periods. The Tertiary period is further divided in to the Paleocene, Eocene, Oligocene, Miocene, and Pliocene epochs.

During this most recent 542 million years, nearly all of the history of life on Earth has unfolded and virtually all of Earth's sedimentary rocks have been created - including most of the sedimentary rocks that now contain oil and natural gas.

# Cambrian Period
# 542 – 488 Million Years Ago

During the Cambrian period the continental plate that later became North America was straddling the equator. The area we know as Texas was situated much as it is today at the margin of the continental plate but it was in the southern hemisphere and much closer to the equator than it is today. Higher sea levels at the time meant that much of the continent including Texas was covered by shallow seas. Beyond the shallow seas of Texas to the south was a wide open and deep ocean. The photograph

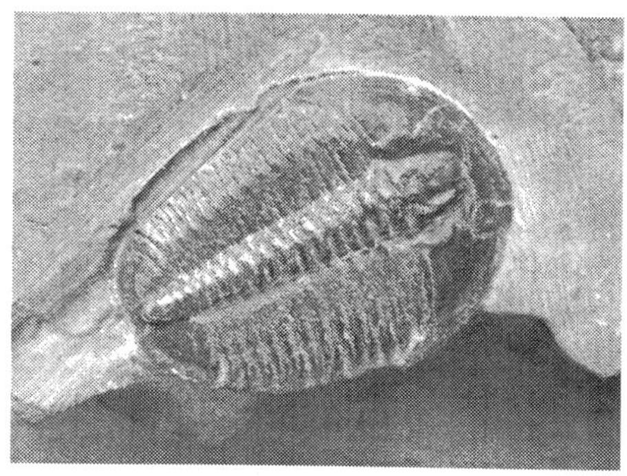

**A trilobite fossil. Trilobites flourished in warm shallow seas during the Cambrian period and continued to live until the end of the Paleozoic era.**

below shows large outcrops of Cambrian age marine sandstone in central Texas. Trilobites flourished in the shallow seas of the Cambrian Period. There are few wells in Texas that produce oil and gas from formations of Cambrian age.

One of the most famous locations of Cambrian fossils is in Canada's Burgess Shale. Animals such as arthropods, corals, brachiopods, mollusks, echinoderms, and sponges appeared during the Cambrian Period. The most

**An outcrop of a massive Cambrian sandstone formation in central Texas.**

famous arthropods to appear during the Cambrian period were trilobites which survived for 300 million years (though the end of the Permian period).

## Ordovician Period
## 488 - 444 Million Years Ago

During the Ordovician period the vast shallow seas of North America continued. Shallow sea plants and animals included corals, echinoderms, anthozoans, bryozoans, algae, brachiopods, cephalopods, gastropods, graptolites, and arthropods like trilobites. The oldest known vertebrate, a fish-like animal called the Astraspis appeared during the Ordovician period. Many organisms such as corals and algae secreted calcium carbonate as part of their biologic processes. Many other organisms held calcium carbonate in their bodies, shells, and skeletons. Over time, calcium carbonate from both living and dead organisms built up on the sea

**This is a rare outcrop of the Ellenburger dolomite formation in central Texas. It was deposited during the Ordovician period. The Ellenburger formation is buried thousands of feet underground throughout most of west Texas. The Ellenburger is a prolific oil and gas producing horizon.**

floor of much of the U.S. over millions of years to form vast thick layers of carbonate sediment.

In Texas, the Ellenburger formation was deposited during the early Ordovician period from just such a process. The Ellenburger formation is a well-known target for oil and gas wells in west

Texas. Outcrops of the Ellenburger can be seen on Texas Highway 71 several miles southeast of Brady, Texas and in the scenic drive through the Franklin Mountains in El Paso. Between those points it is buried thousands of feet below the surface.

Beyond of the shallow seas of Texas was deep ocean. Dry land existed in what is today the northern part of North America. The dry land portions of the continental plates were still relatively barren but some arthropods began to move out of the water and colonize the land during the Ordovician period. The limestone that would later become the present-day peak of Mount Everest was deposited in a shallow marine sea during the Ordovician period. But it would be over 300 million more years before the Indian plate began to collide with the Eurasian plate to push up the Himalayas and create Mount Everest.

# Silurian Period
# 444 - 416 Million Years Ago

The waters at Niagara Falls are falling across Silurian dolomites that were laid down in shallow tropical seas. Sea levels rose and fell many times during the Silurian period as shallow seas continued to cover much of North America and Texas. The North American plate was moving slowly northward. The first vascular plants were appearing on land. Corals were flourishing in the seas. Jawless fishes were the most common vertebrates; but the earliest jawed fishes also appeared during the Silurian. Other animals included anthozoans, brachiopods, bryozoans, cephalopods, bivalves, echinoderms, graptolites, and arthropods. Limestone, dolomite, and chert formations including the oil and gas productive Fusselman formation in west Texas were deposited in shallow marine seas during the early Silurian period.

# Devonian Period
# 416 - 359 Million Years Ago

Sometimes called the "Age of Fish", the Devonian period brought an increase in the numbers and diversity of fish in the seas. Amphibians appeared for the first time. The Devonian also brought terrestrial plants including ferns and the first wide spread forests of tall trees. Shales, sandstones, limestone, and chert were deposited in west Texas. The Woodford shale was deposited during the latter part of the Devonian period.

# Mississippian Period
# 359 - 318 Million Years Ago

Shallow seas continued to cover Texas during the Mississippian period. In the seas, corals, anthozoans, brachiopods, bryozoans, cephalopods, bivalves, echinoderms, gastropods, and arthropods continued to flourish. On land huge forests were exploding across the landscape. The gas-productive Barnett shale was deposited during the latter part of the Mississippian period.

## Pennsylvanian Period 318 – 299 Million Years Ago

The Pennsylvanian period was an exciting time. Life was flourishing on land and in the seas.

Four-legged aquatic reptile-like animals began to walk on land. Giant clubmoss trees and a wide array of ferns filled vast warm swamps on land. The organic matter produced in the swamps formed peat bogs that were later buried under many layers of sediment and converted under heat and pressure to form the bituminous coal that is mined in much of the world today.

**A Pennsylvanian-age fossil of a sea sponge that lived in a shallow sea in north central Texas. This delicate fossil has survived for over 300 million years.**

Note: Outside the United States, the Mississippian and Pennsylvanian periods are often lumped together and referred to as the Carboniferous period.

Fish and other marine vertebrates continued to develop in the seas covering much of the continental plates. Marine life was abundant in the warm shallow seas. Thick sections of limestone with lesser amounts of sandstone and shale were deposited in west Texas and north central Texas. Numerous oil and gas wells produce from Pennsylvanian age rocks deposited in west Texas and north central Texas during the Pennsylvanian period. These include from top to bottom the Cisco, Canyon, Strawn, and Bend formations.

**Pennsylvanian limestone outcrop. This oil and gas producing formation is buried throughout most of west Texas and north central Texas.**

**An outcrop of limestone deposited during the Pennsylvanian period in north Texas. Thousands of wells have produced oil and gas from Pennsylvainan limestones.**

## Ouachita Orogeny

Approximately 300 million years ago, near the end of the Pennsylvanian period, the North American continent collided with another continent along its southern margin. This collision pushed up rocks of Cambrian through Pennsylvanian age to create a mountain range called the Ouachita Mountains. The mountain range extended diagonally across Texas from present day Del Rio, through Waco and Dallas, and in to Oklahoma and then east in to Arkansas. While this mountain range has been completely eroded in Texas, its remnants can still be seen in Oklahoma and Arkansas. At the present time, oil and gas reservoirs are extremely sparse within the area that was once covered by the mountains.

Although it is not important for petroleum geology, it is interesting to note that because of the top soil differences on either side of the eroded Ouachita range in Texas, oak trees are prevalent only on the southeast side of the band while mesquite plants are more typical on the northwest side of the range.

The uplifting of the Ouachita Mountains across Texas also caused a downward movement of the west Texas and north central Texas regions that were north and west of the newly formed Ouachita Mountains. Several basins (bowl shaped regions) were formed in these areas which included the oil and gas productive basins of west Texas and north central Texas.

Sediments subsequently filled these basins during the Permian period that followed (299 – 251 Million Years Ago). The Ouachita Mountains permanently divided Texas in to three distinct petroleum regions. The area in Texas to the north and west of the Ouachita Mountains produces primarily from Paleozoic rocks. The area where the Ouachita Mountains existed and eroded produces virtually no oil and gas. And the area to the southeast of the Ouachita's produces primarily from younger sediments that were not deposited until after the continental plates began to pull apart later in the

Triassic period. All of the productive formations in East Texas and along Texas' gulf coast are Mesozoic and Cenozoic in age.

## Permian Period 299 – 251 Million Years Ago

The final period of the Paleozoic Era was the Permian period. During this time North America, South America, Africa, India, Antarctica, and Australia were all combined in to one supercontinent. Ferns and conifers continued to thrive on land. Cycads very similar to present-day cycads appeared for the first time. Early reptile-like animals were abundant. Calcareous algae, anthozoans, bryozoans, bivalves, brachiopods, cephalopods, and echinoderms lived in the seas. The huge reef at El Capitan in west Texas was formed during the Permian period. The bowl-shaped region known as the Permian basin was filled with thousands of feet of sediment during the Permian period. Today it is the largest petroleum producing basin in the lower 48 states.

During the Permian period much of Texas was covered by warm shallow seas just as it had been throughout most of the 290 Million-Year-Long Paleozoic Era.

The Paleozoic era yielded thousands of feet of organic-rich sediment. The end of the Permian period was marked by the most severe extinction event the Earth has ever seen. Approximately 90% of all species on Earth at that time went extinct. A series of volcanic eruptions in Siberia that lasted for over a million years is suspected to have altered the oceans and the atmosphere enough to cause the extinctions. These eruptions produced thousands of cubic miles of basalt that still exist today. They are the Siberian Traps.

# Triassic Period 251-200 Million Years Ago

The Triassic Period followed the great extinction at the end of the Permian Period. The continents were still combined in a single super-continent called Pangaea. South America, North America, Africa, and Europe were all pressed together. There was no Atlantic Ocean. Antarctica, India, and Australia were combined along the southeast side of Africa; and Asia extended north from Europe over the north pole. But toward the end of the Triassic Period Pangaea began to break apart in to the smaller continents we have today. The Atlantic Ocean began to form as North America and South America began to move away from Africa and Europe. The Gulf of Mexico was born during this time as North America and South America began to pull apart. Mammals, dinosaurs, crocodiles, and turtles began to evolve. The Triassic was the first period that saw a large number of land-dwelling dinosaur species. Some of the first flying reptiles appeared. Conifer and cycads also grew and numerous new species arrived.

## Jurassic Period
## 200-146 Million Years Ago

The breaking apart of Pangaea continued. The Gulf of Mexico widened and parts of the Rocky Mountains were being pushed up. The Gulf of Mexico was a depression in the Earth's surface that was not yet connected to the world's oceans. It occasionally dried out leaving vast salt plains. One such salt deposit is the Louann Salt. It is the source of the salt domes along the gulf coast. Large dinosaurs were in their prime during the Jurassic and the subsequent Cretaceous Period. The oceans were full of life.

# Cretaceous Period
# 146 - 65.5 Million Years Ago

The breakup of Pangaea progressed and the continents continued to move toward their present day positions. At times, sea levels were hundreds of feet higher during the Cretaceous period and the global climate was warm. Flowering plants evolved and dinosaurs continued their dominance of the land. Shallow seas covered much of what is continental dry land in North America today.

**These dinosaur foot prints were left in mudstone from the Cretaceous period in north Texas.**

The Cretaceous period ended 65.5 million years ago. At the time, a long series of eruptions on the Indian plate produced the Deccan Traps in present-day India. The Deccan Traps are an area that was covered with igneous rock during the eruptions. There was also a meteor impact that produced the Chicxulub crater at the tip of the Yucatán peninsula. The eruptions in India and the meteor impact are suspected in the extinction of the dinosaurs and other species and bringing an end to the Cretaceous period and the Mesozoic era.

## Tertiary Period
## 65.5 - 2.6 Million Years Ago

Continents continued to spread. The Atlantic Ocean continued to widen. The continents began to look like they do today. It was during the Tertiary Period that the Indian plate collided with Asia and pushed up the Himalayan Mountains. The Tertiary Period is sometimes broken in to two periods called the Paleogene Period and the Neogene Period. In the Gulf Coast of the United States where Tertiary sandstone deposits are productive oil and gas reservoirs, this time is usually referred to as the Tertiary Period. The Tertiary Period is broken in to five smaller epochs known as the Paleocene, Eocene, Oligocene, Miocene, and Pliocene. Refer to the Geologic Time Scale on page 43 for a clear picture. The dinosaurs were gone. But most plant life survived from the Cretaceous to the Tertiary. On land, mammals grew in size and in diversity.

Along the gulf coast, thick formations of sandstone and shale were deposited as tiny fragments of rocks were eroded in inland areas and transported by water across the coastal areas and out in to the basin in the Gulf of Mexico. Tertiary formations deepen and thicken as you move from the Ouachita orogenic belt southeastward out it to the Gulf of

Mexico. Along the coastline of Texas and about four or five counties inward from the present-day coast are the areas in Texas where you will find Tertiary deposits within drillable depths. All of the existing offshore oil and gas reservoirs in the Gulf of Mexico are Tertiary in age. Near the coastline, it is impossible to drill through the Tertiary formations and in to the Cretaceous. But as you move inland toward San Antonio, Austin, and College Station, the Tertiary deposits are thinner and shallower so it is possible to drill through them and in to upper Cretaceous formations.

For more information about Petroleum Geology, visit the American Association of Petroleum Geologists' web site at

www.aapg.org

# Chapter 3 Finding a Prospect

The two most common methods of locating promising places to drill wells are through seismic surveying and by studying the information gained from previously drilled wells. We will discuss both of these methods in this chapter.

## Seismic Surveying

Seismic surveying is an operation where compressional waves from an energy source on the surface are sent down in to the Earth's subsurface. The compressional waves reflect off of the surfaces of underground formations. Technically speaking there is a reflection any time a compressional wave reaches a point where there is a change in acoustic impedance. When the reflected waves return to the surface the ground moves up and down in very small amounts. The ground movements caused by the arrival of the reflected waves are detected by small devices placed on the surface called geophones. These geophones are very similar to the geophones that are used to detect earthquakes. The output voltages of the geophones are recorded on computers. The plots of output voltages from the geophones versus time are later interpreted to identify structures of subsurface formations that may be trapping oil and gas. Seismic data can also be used to obtain clues as to the nature of the fluid in the pores of those formations - be they liquid or gas.

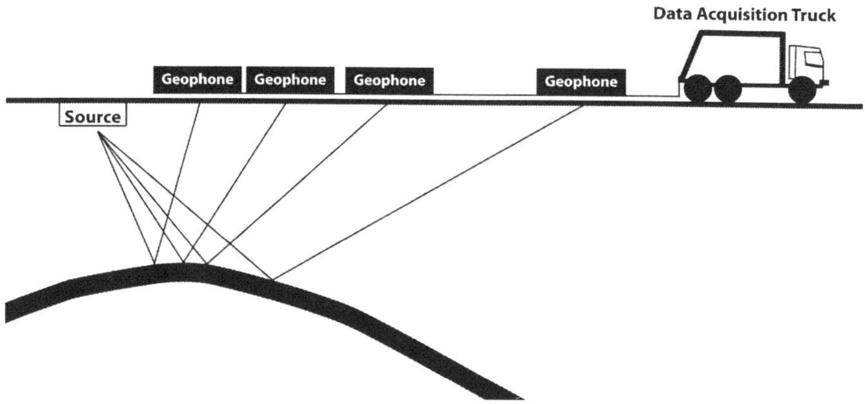


**Seismic Surveying Operation**

**Energy from a source at the surface is reflected off of underground formations and is detected by an array of geophones which send signals to computers in a data acquisition truck where they are recorded for subsequent analysis.**

**A vibroseis truck uses a heavy steel plate that vibrates against the ground to provide a source of seismic energy.**

Seismic data never hurts but it also never provides certainty as to whether or not a structure contains hydrocarbons; and it does not provide certainty as to whether the fluid in the pore space of a formation is a liquid or a gas.

The energy source that provides the compressional waves necessary to acquire seismic data can be created in several ways. The four most common methods on land are:

(1) Dynamite Buried Underground
(2) Vibroseis Trucks
(3) Air Guns in a Water Pit
(4) Weight Drops

Small amounts of dynamite are usually buried in a shallow boreholes about 100 feet below the surface. Electric wires extend to the surface which allow the seismic contractor to set off the dynamite when the geophones are in place and the computer is recording their signals.

The next method for creating compressional waves at the surface is using vibroseis trucks. Vibroseis trucks (also known as Vibe Trucks) use a very heavy steel plate that vibrates against the ground under the force of hydraulics from the truck. The frequency of the vibration is controlled by the truck. Seismic contractors typically perform a "sweep" of vibrations from a low frequency to a high frequency. A typical vibration sweep lasts for about 6-10 seconds.

Air guns are used for all offshore seismic surveys but they can also be used on land if they are placed in an earthen pit of water. Air guns use a cylinder of compressed air that is is suddenly released to create a powerful compressional wave.

Dropping a heavy weight on the ground can also provide a source of seismic energy; and there are trucks that do this.

# Subsurface Control

Subsurface control refers to the knowledge you have about subsurface formations from previously drilled wells. By observing the depths of a particular formation in various wells, a three-dimensional image of the formation can be developed. You can determine the structure and dip of a subsurface formation by interpolating between known points on the formation's surface. In the United States, much of the geologic and production information from previously drilled wells is in the public domain. By combining your knowledge of the structure and dip of a formation with production data from the wells that have produced from that formation, you can identify promising places to drill new wells. Petroleum Geologists use all of their knowledge of geology and all of the subsurface information they can gather to find new oil fields or new locations within existing oilfields.

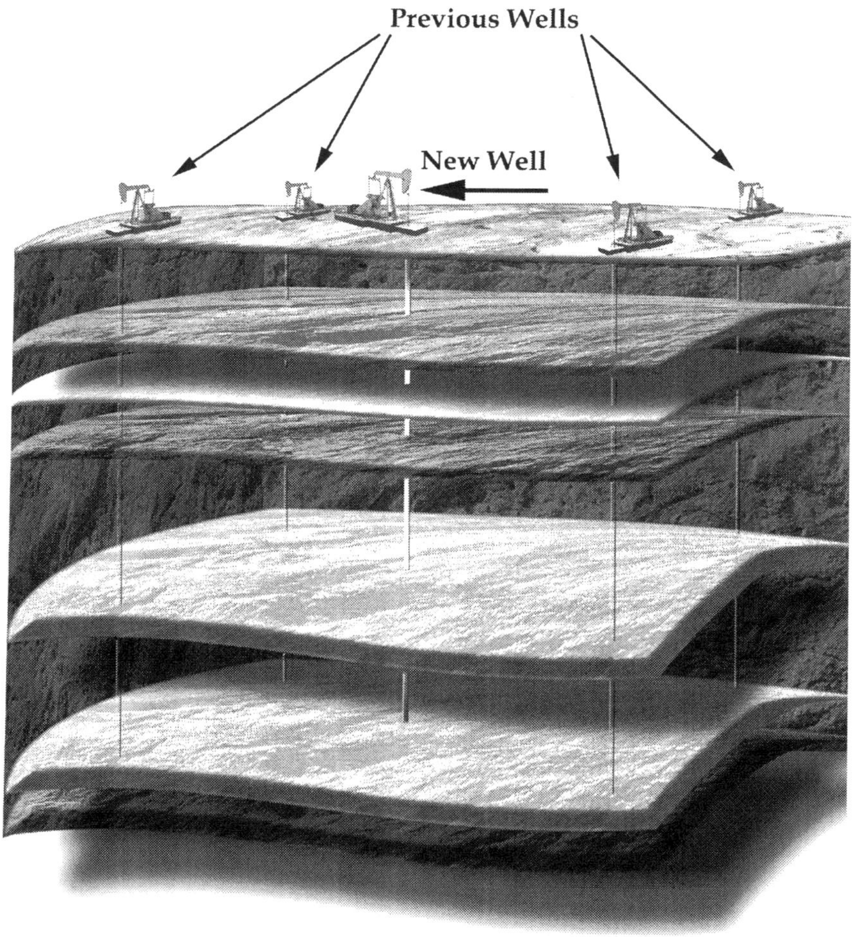


**This diagrams shows how a new oil well can be drilled near or between previously drilled oil wells using information gained from those wells. This information is called subsurface control. As expected, the new well in the center of the field successfully penetrated the same pay zones as the four previously drilled wells.**

# Political Considerations

When searching for oil and gas, the United States offers the lowest political risk of any nation on Earth.

The U.S. is extraordinary among other reasons because most mineral interests are privately owned. This means you can quickly and easily acquire mineral interests through simple negotiations with private individuals. The states and the federal governement do own some mineral interests because they own the minerals under government land. Leases can still be aquired in these areas with a few bureaucratic hurdles. Acquiring state leases is far easier than acquiring federal leases.

The opportunities to lease private and state land in the United States far surpass those of other countries where acquiring

exploration rights requires orders of magnitude more cash and time.
The whole process of negotiating and signing an oil and gas lease with an individual can take less than a month and require a few thousand to hundreds of thousands of dollars.

## Oil & Gas Producing Regions in the United States of America

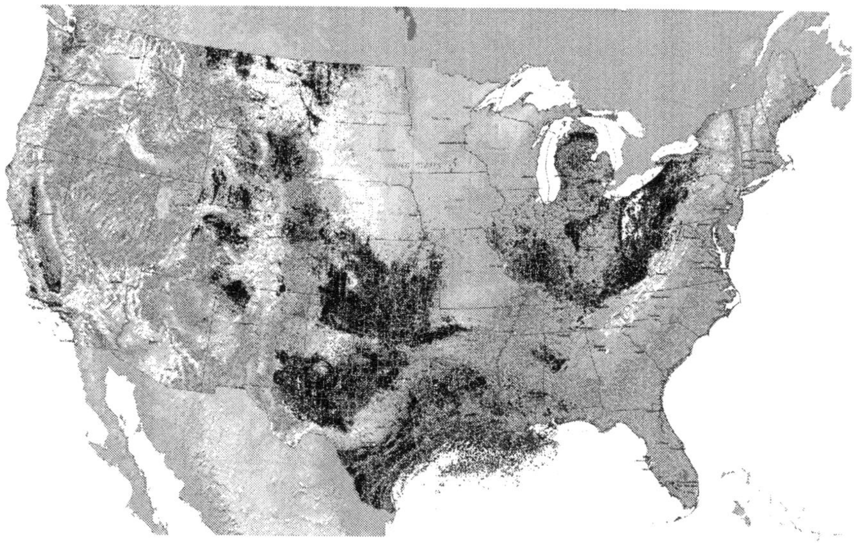

**The areas shown in black represent current and historical oil and natural gas producing areas in the United States. You are more likely to find oil or natural gas in the black areas than outside of the black areas. (Source: USGS)**

# Chapter 4 Drilling a Well

In this chapter we will discuss how a drilling rig is used to drill a well.

## Positioning a Drilling Rig to Drill a New Well

In addition to being situated above or near an oil and gas reservoir, a drilling rig and its wellbore must be located within the oil and gas lease premises and outside any restricted areas that may have been designated within the lease. As an example, some leases require that no wells are drilled within 200 feet of an existing house, barn, or water well. The spacing requirements for new wells and the minimum distances between a well's surface location and the lease lines and any other wells are given by the state regulatory agency; and they depend on the depth of the well to be drilled.

## Deviated Wells

If there is an obstruction on the surface above a prospective reservoir target, such as a lake, such that an Operator (an oil company) cannot place a drilling rig directly above the target, then a drilling rig can be placed at a nearby location and a deviated wellbore can be drilled which follows

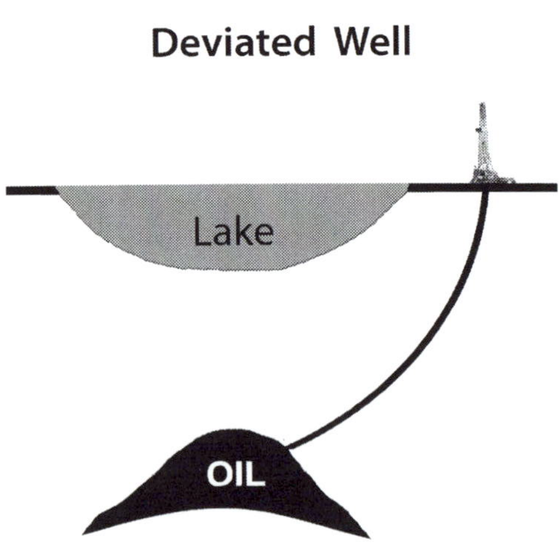

a curved path underground back to the prospective target that is directly beneath the obstruction. Drilling deviated wells costs more than drilling vertical wells and special considerations may be required during the production phase.

Beyond that, flat land is better than steeply sloping land and dry land is better than mud; but neither of these will stop a determined group of investors.

## Drilling Permit

With an oil and gas lease in place, an application for a permit to drill a well can be submitted to the state oil and gas regulatory agency. The permit application will describe the proposed location of the well, the lease boundaries, and the intended geologic targets. Permit applications usually require a small fee of a few hundred dollars. It can take anywhere from a few days to a few weeks to receive a permit.

# Drilling and Spacing Unit

The regulatory agency will establish the "drilling and spacing unit" for the well. The drilling and spacing unit is the amount of land area that must be dedicated to a particular well. Typical drilling and spacing units are 40 acres, 80 acres, 160 acres, 320 acres or 640 acres. The size of the drilling and spacing unit depends on the depth of the well and the formation. Deeper wells generally require more acreage. The origin of this rule comes from the notion that oil and gas reserves can best be developed without waste by drilling one and only one well within an area that one well is capable of draining.

## Surveyor's Plat

The application for a drilling permit will include a Surveyor's plat of the proposed surface location and the bottom hole location if the well will be deviated or horizontal. The plat will show the lease boundaries and the distance from the proposed well location to the nearest lease boundary line. The application will also include the projected total depth of the well. If the well will be drilled in a new area or to an unexplored depth it will be designated as a wildcat well. If the well will serve to develop a known reservoir it will be designated as a development well.

## Drilling Contractors

Few oil companies own their own drilling rigs. So when oil companies are ready to drill wells they seek the services of a drilling contractor. Drilling contractors own drilling rigs and employ the skilled personnel who are required to operate them. The oil company and the drilling contractor discuss the equipment, procedures, and the wellbore specifications that the oil company requires and then the two parties enter into a contract to drill the well.

## Day Rate

The contract may specify a fixed cost per day for the use of the drilling rig and a competent crew. The oil company will direct the day-to-day operations of the rig and will be billed a day rate regardless of the progress that is made in drilling the well on any given day. This arrangement is known as a day rate contract. The oil company will have a person at the drill site at all times to direct the drilling contractor. This person is called the company representative and may be an employee of the oil company or a drilling consultant. This person has day-to-day decision-making authority while the well is being drilled. The deeper or more complex a well is to drill, the more likely it will be contracted on a day rate.

## Turnkey

If a well is relatively shallow and the drilling procedures and parameters required to successfully drill a well are well-known, then some drilling contractors are willing to provide a turnkey contract. Under this arrangement, the drilling contractor must successfully drill a well to the depth prescribed in the contract before payment is due from the oil company. This eliminates much of the operational risk of drilling a well for the oil company and limits its cost. The highest ranking person on the drilling contractor's crew is called the Tool Pusher. Under a turnkey contract the Tool Pusher has day-to-day decision making authority while the well is being drilled.

For more information about drilling contractors, visit the International Association of Drilling Contractor's web site at www.iadc.org.

## Staking the Location

The first step in drilling a well is to place a stake in the ground at the intended location. This is a simple piece of wood or a metal rod. Having a Surveyor's stake at the location insures that the well is drilled in the intended location and meets the placement requirements of the state oil and gas regulatory agency. This step is usually performed by the same Surveyor that prepared the plat that was submitted with the drilling permit application.

Once the stake is in the ground, the drilling contractor will begin preparing the location around the stake for the drilling rig. The immediate area around the stake needs to be made clear and level. A water well may be drilled at the edge of the location to provide water to use during the drilling operation. Earthen pits may be dug to create mud pits and/or a reserve pit. Large drilling rigs that are used to drill deep wells usually have a large earthen reserve pit with metal tanks for mud tanks. Smaller drilling rigs drilling shallower wells may have a similar arrangement or they may have earthen pits for their drilling fluid. Preparing a location for a drilling rig should take no more than two weeks.

# Drilling Rigs

## Cable Tool Drilling Rigs

During the 1800's, oil wells were drilled with cable tool drilling rigs. A cable tool rig uses cable to lower a cable tool bit in to a hole. A cable tool bit is a simple heavy bar with a pointed end on the bottom. The cable is connected to the top of the bit and extends to the rig at the surface. The cable tool rig is used to repeatedly raise the bit a few feet and then drop it and allow it to impact the rock at the bottom of the wellbore. This repeated raising and dropping of the bit causes the rock at the bottom of the wellbore to be crushed in to small fragments. The cable tool bit is then pulled out of the hole by using the cable. Next, a device known as a bailer is lowered to the bottom of the wellbore using a cable. A bailer is essentially a hollow pipe with a trap door on the bottom. Its purpose is to collect the rock fragments that were generated by the crushing action of the bit. The bailer is raised and dropped repeatedly just like the bit. Each time the bailer falls on the rock fragments at the bottom of the wellbore, some of them enter the bailer through a one-way trap door. When most of the fragments have been collected, the bailer is hoisted back to the surface by the cable. Then the bit is again lowered to the bottom of the wellbore. With the rock fragments from the previous trip in the hole removed, the bit is free to begin pummeling fresh rock at a slightly deeper depth. By repeated employing alternating use of a bit to crush rock and a bailer to remove the crushed rock, the wellbore is gradually deepened. This process is called cable tool drilling. Cable tool drilling is relatively slow when compared to rotary drilling. Most of the wells drilled in the late 1800's and early 1900's employed cable tool rigs. Notably the Spindletop gusher of 1901 was drilled with a rotary drilling rig. By the 1940's the dominant drilling method was rotary drilling. And the dominance of rotary drilling continues through today.

## Rotary Drilling Rigs

A rotary drilling rig uses a rotating drill bit at the bottom of a length of pipe to scrape and cut through subsurface rock and create a wellbore. Rotary drilling rigs have three primary systems: (1) a rotary system that rotates the drill pipe and the drill bit, (2) a circulating system that pumps drilling fluid down the inside of the drill pipe and back up to the surface through the space between the outside of the drill pipe and the borehole wall, and (3) a hoisting system that is used to raise and lower equipment such as drill pipe and casing into and out of the wellbore. The hoisting system is also used to hold tension on the drill pipe while drilling so that it stays straight and does not buckle.

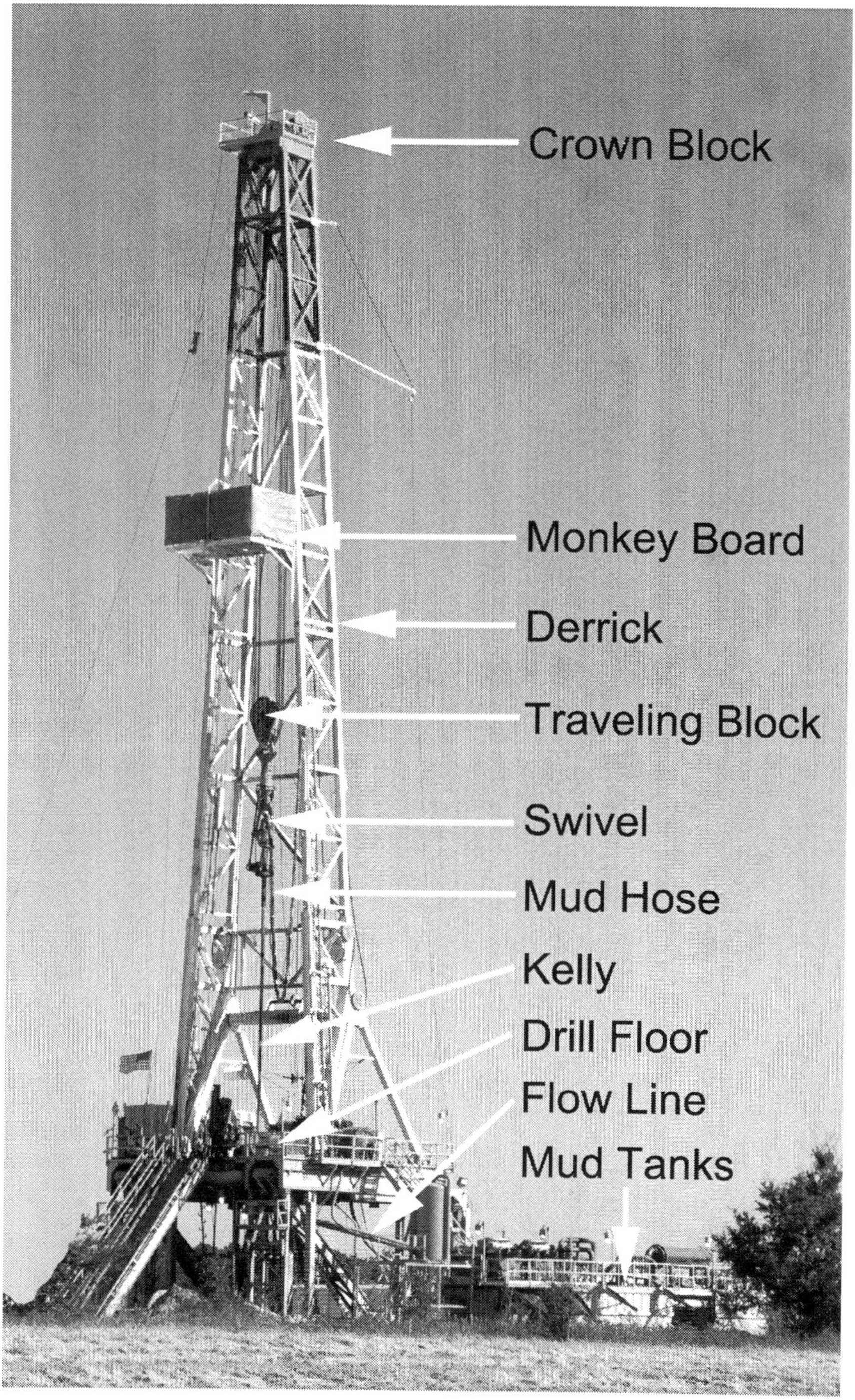


**Rotary Drilling Rig**

# Rotary System

The rotary system consists of the drill bit, drill collars, drill pipe, a kelly joint, a kelly bushing, and a rotary table. The pipe that is used to rotate the drill bit is known as drill pipe or drill stem. It is usually constructed in 30-foot long segments known as joints. Multiple joints of drill pipe connected together in one long string in a well are together known as a drill string.

**Drill pipe on a pipe rack adjacent to a drilling rig. These joints of drill pipe are about to be picked up and screwed together to make a drill string.**

Part of the weight of the drill string above the drill bit exerts a downward force on the drill bit which increases the penetration rate as the bit turns. Often a few segments of extra

## Drilling Rig Rotary System

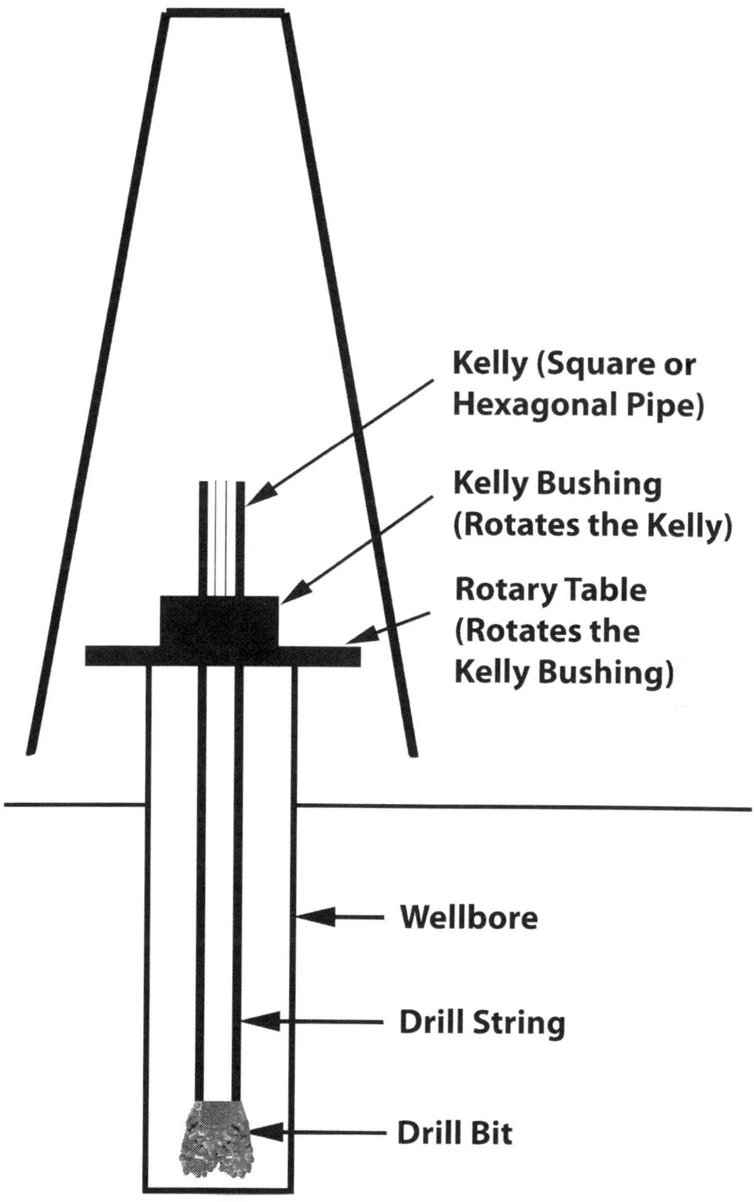

large and very heavy joints of drill pipe are placed in the drill string just above the drill bit. These joints of especially heavy pipe are known as drill collars or heavy weights. They provide weight on the bit which increases the penetration rate. The drill bit is turned by rotating the drill pipe at the surface. A special joint of pipe called a kelly joint is used at the surface. Rather than being round in cross-section like most pipe, a kelly joint is square or hexagonal in cross-section. The square or hexagonal shape of the pipe makes it easier to clench than round pipe. Just as a wrench is designed to turn a nut, there is special wrench of sorts on a drilling rig that is designed to turn the kelly. It is called the kelly bushing. The kelly bushing wraps tightly around the flat surfaces of the kelly joint the same way that a wrench wraps around a nut. The kelly bushing rests on a flat spinning surface called a rotary table. The rotary table is turned by way of linkage to a motor.

When the rotary table turns it turns the kelly bushing. As the kelly bushing turns it turns the kelly joint. And as the kelly joint turns it turns the drill string below it. And as the drill string turns it turns the drill bit. As the drill bit turns the well is drilled.

# Rotary Drill Bits

Tri-Cone Drill Bit (Side View)

Tri-Cone Drill Bit (Bottom View)

Rotary Drill bits are available in two broad groups: rolling cutter bits and drag bits. The most common rolling cutter bits are tri-cone rolling cutter bits. Tri-cone rolling cutter bits have three rolling cones with teeth mounted on them that roll on the rock at the bottom of the wellbore to crush, grind, and scrape the rock. The drilling fluid flows out through jets at high pressure and cleans the cuttings away from the cutting face of the rock.

Polycrystalline Diamond Compact Bit (PDC Bit)

Drag bits have no moving parts. They have fixed blades finished with extremely strong metal alloys. Sometimes the blades have industrial diamonds inserted on them that assist in tearing the rock as the bit turns. Such drill bits are called PDC bits.The number of blades on a drag bit typically ranges from two to seven. The choice of a drill bit depends on the type of rock that will be drilled and the amount of footage that the Operator intends to drill through. A drill bit may be purchased from a bit manufacturer or rented. If rented, the price is usually for an agreed amount per foot that the drill bit is used to drill.

To summarize the rotary system on a rotary drilling rig, a stationary motor on the drilling rig turns a series of gears and linkages which turns the rotary table which turns the Kelly bushing which acts as a wrench which rotates the top joint of drill pipe known as the Kelly which in turn rotates all of the joints of drill pipe connected below the Kelly which rotates the drill bit which cuts through the rock and creates a wellbore.

## Circulating System

As the drill bit turns it breaks the rock in its path in to small pieces. The small pieces of rock are known as cuttings. Cuttings must be removed from the wellbore or they will accumulate and impede the progress of the drill bit. In order to remove the cuttings, a liquid is pumped down the inside of the drill pipe while the drill bit is turning.

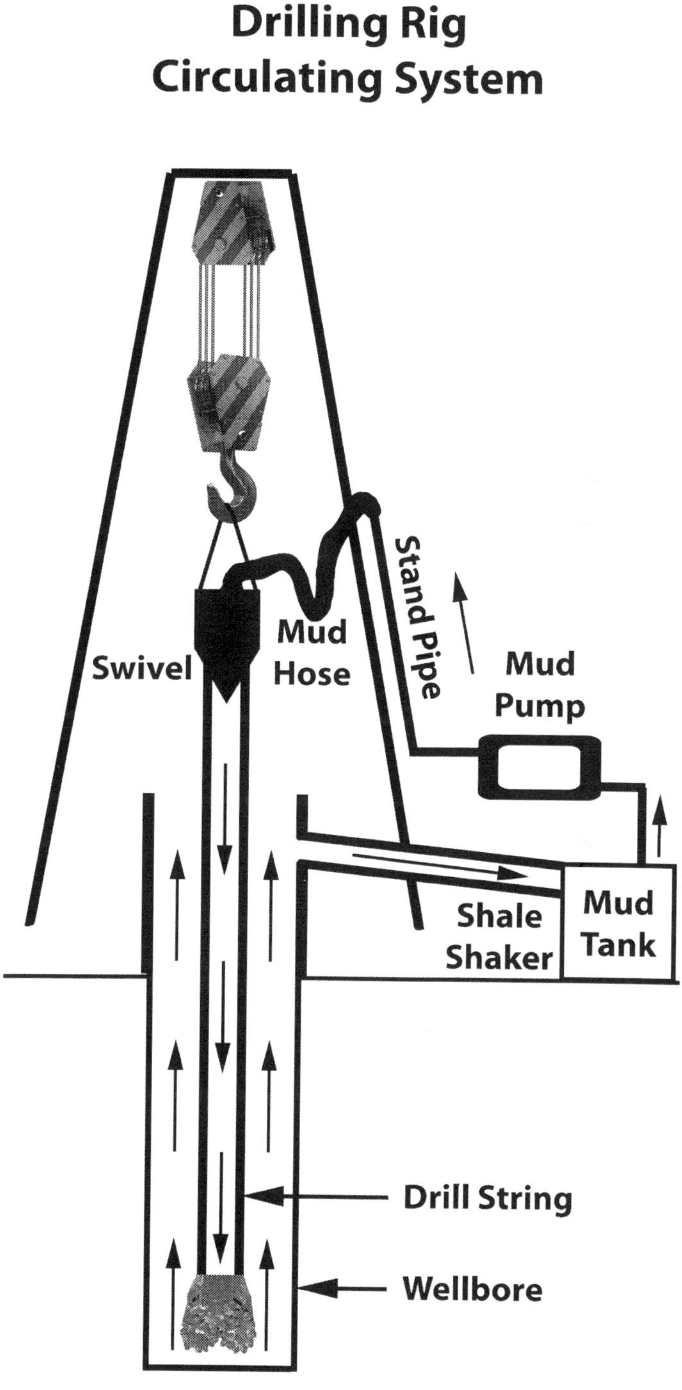
Drilling Rig
Circulating System
Swivel
Mud
Hose
Stand Pipe
Mud
Pump
Shale
Shaker
Mud
Tank
Drill String
Wellbore

The liquid is known as drilling fluid or drilling mud. The drilling fluid exits at the bottom of the drill string through special holes in the drill bit. The drilling fluid exits these holes (or jets) at high pressure much like water exits a wand at a car wash. The high-pressure streams of drilling fluid exiting the drill bit clean the cutting surface so that the drill bit is always crushing and scraping new rock. After the fluid exits the bit and cleans the cutting face of the rock it returns to the surface by moving up the space in the wellbore that is outside the drill pipe. This space between the borehole wall and the outside of the drill pipe is known as the annulus. The drilling fluid must have sufficient viscosity and upward velocity to lift the cuttings of rock up to the surface. Once at the surface the cuttings are separated out of the drilling fluid and the remaining clean drilling fluid is again pumped down the inside of the drill pipe, out the jets in the drill bit, and then back up the annulus.

A device known as a shale shaker removes the cuttings from the drilling fluid at the surface.

The system of pumps, hoses, and pipes that allow this continuous circulation of fluid to take place is known as the circulating system. A special piece of equipment known as a swivel is placed at the top of the drill string which allows fluid to be pumped in to the top of the kelly joint even while it is rotating.

## Drilling Fluid

Drilling fluid is part of the circulating system. It is designed to offset the pressure of downhole formation fluids, lift cuttings to the surface, cool and lubricate the bit, and minimize the odds of the hole collapsing while drilling operations are in progress.

Perhaps the most sensitive formations encountered while drilling are clays in shales. Special care is given to use drilling fluids that are not likely to react with clays because clays that react with drilling fluids can slough off in to the borehole and cause problems. Numerous additives are available to control the density, viscosity, reactivity, fluid loss, and fluid mechanical properties of the drilling fluid. In challenging wells, the drilling fluid contractor will provide a Mud Engineer who stays on location while the well is being drilled. The Mud Engineer constantly monitors the composition and properties of the drilling fluid and makes changes when necessary.

## Hoisting System

When the drill bit reaches the desired depth it must be removed from the wellbore along with all of the drill pipe above it. A string of drill pipe in a well bore weighs many thousands of pounds. So a drilling rig includes a hoisting

# Drilling Rig Hoisting System

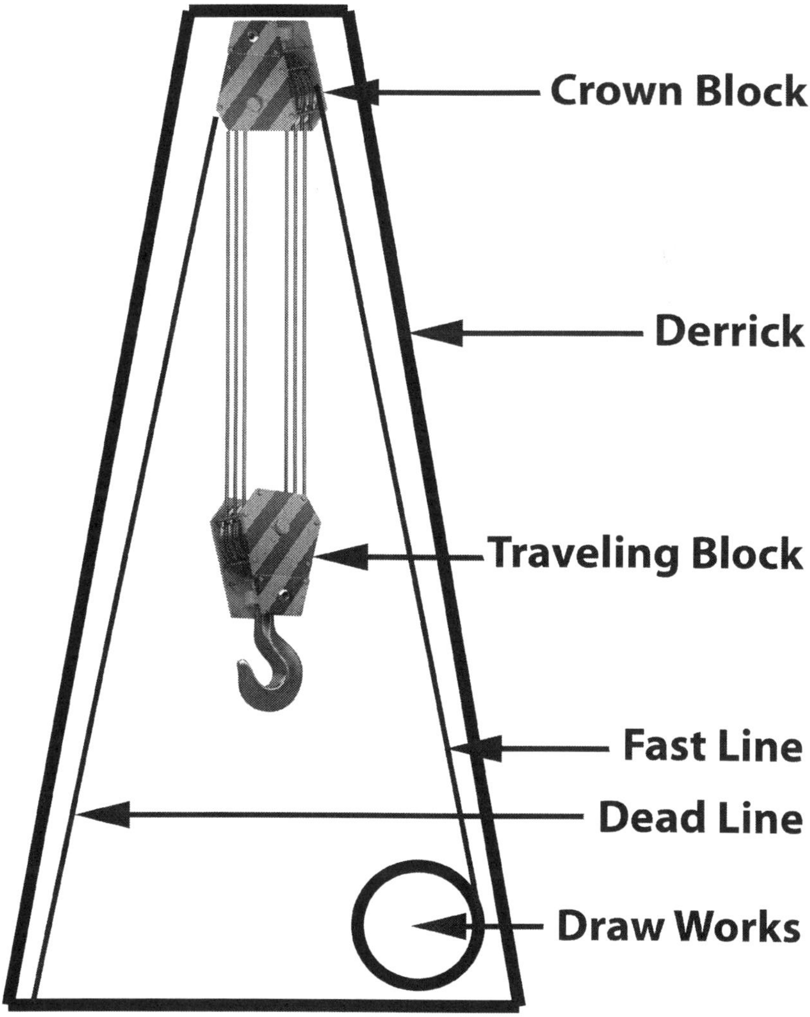

system to lift the drill pipe out of the hole. It operates like a crane for the well.

The well-known derrick portion of a drilling rig provides the vertical structure needed to lift the drill string out of the hole. A block and tackle with a hook similar to a crane's hook is used to lift the drill string and to hold tension on the drill string while drilling. The hoisting system is also used to run casing in to a well. The hoisting system must be strong enough to support the weight of drill strings and casing strings. But it must also be strong enough to withstand the additional stress exerted when a string of pipe becomes stuck and the Driller is attempting to free them by jerking them up and down using the hoisting system. It can be quite an experience if you are on the drill floor while this is happening. The hook load varies by many tens of thousands of pounds over very short time intervals as the Driller pulls high tension on the drill string and then releases it suddenly in an effort to jar the string free. Things shake. A lot.

## Casing

After the drill bit reaches the desired depth and the drill bit and drill pipe are removed from the well bore, a string of metal pipe known as casing may be placed in the wellbore. Casing is pipe that is placed in the wellbore to permanently hold the wellbore open. It prevents the collapse of the wellbore during and after the drilling operation and it hydraulically isolates fluids in the wellbore from fluids in the rock formations that the well has penetrated. Joints of casing may be run all the way to the total depth (TD) of the well or they may be set some distance above the bottom of the well. Casing diameter ranges from over 20 inches to as small as 2-7/8 inches. Individual joints of casing are typically 40 feet long. The American Petroleum Institute has developed

**Casing on a rack at a casing supplier's yard**

standards for casing as well as other oilfield equipment and procedures. API grades of casing inform an Engineer of the minimum yield strengths and minimum tensile strengths for various casing products. Visit www.api.org.

Wells are often drilled in several phases using different sizes of drill bits and casing in each phase. The Operator will begin with the largest bit size first, then set casing, and then use a smaller bit that will fit inside the previous casing to drill the next section of the well. The largest and shallowest casing is called conductor pipe. Next is the surface casing. Surface casing is often set to a depth specified by the state regulatory agency to protect fresh water aquifers. Fresh water aquifers are most common at very shallow depths. The next string of casing is intermediate casing. Most shallow wells do not require any intermediate casing. Deeper wells may require one or more intermediate strings of casing. The last string of casing is called the production string or production casing. It will only be run if the Operator will attempt a completion in the deepest section of the well.

## Example Casing Program

An Operator may begin with 50 feet of 20-inch conductor pipe.

The surface section could be drilled

from 50 feet to 1,000 feet using a 17-1/2 inch drill bit. Then 13-3/8 surface casing could be run in the well to 1,000 feet.

A 12-1/4 inch drill bit could be run inside the 13-3/8 inch surface casing to drill the intermediate section from 1,000 feet to 9,000 feet. Then 10-3/4 inch intermediate casing would be run in the well to 9,000 feet.

Afterward a 9-7/8 inch bit could be used to drill the TD section from 9,000 feet to 12,000 feet.

Finally 7-1/2 inch production casing could be run from ground level to TD at 12,000 feet.

Regardless of its size, the casing that is set at the well's total depth is called the production casing or the production string. The bottom of the casing is called the casing shoe.

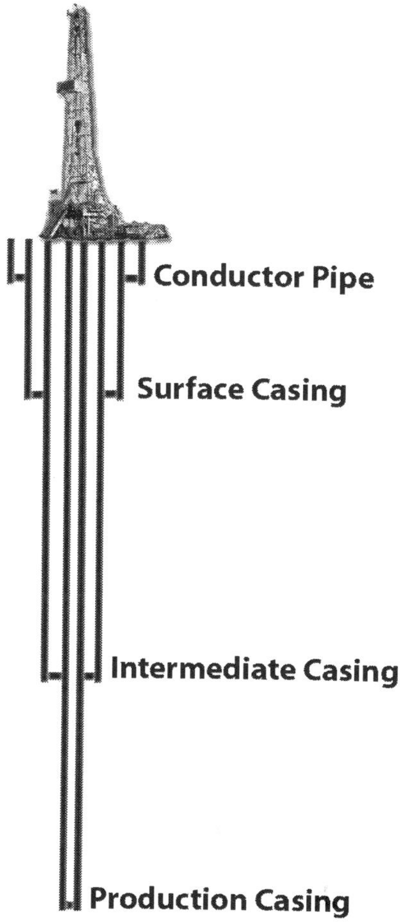


Generally speaking, deeper wells have more sections and require more casing strings. Any casing strings that are set after the surface casing (which is first) and before the production string (which is last) are called intermediate casing strings. Intermediate casing strings may be set when an Operator is transitioning from drilling in relatively low pressure shallow zones to higher pressure deeper zones. Drilling fluids with high density may be required to offset the deeper over-pressured zones. But drilling fluids with high mud weights may exceed the fracture gradient at shallower depths. So it may be impossible to drill with a mud that is of sufficient density to offset deep high-pressure zones without inadvertently fracturing (breaking down) shallower formations and losing drilling fluid in to those shallower zones. These problems can be exacerbated when drilling through deeper zones that are also kicking and well control procedures must be used. And thus it is sometimes necessary to set intermediate casing when using higher mud weights so that shallow formations are not broken down.

## Cementing

Each time a string of casing is set in the hole, cement is placed in the space between the outside of the casing and the borehole wall. This space is known as the annulus and the presence of cement in the annulus creates a hydraulic seal that prevents fluids in the rock formations from entering the borehole, traveling from one zone to another, or traveling to the surface. Cementing is a service provided by specialized cement pumping contractors. Engineers in the oil company and the pumping contractor carefully select the components of the cement slurry for each section of the well. Variables such as density, viscosity, compressive strength, and curing time are important. The cement slurry must be of sufficient density to offset the reservoir fluid pressure while the cement is being pumped in to place. It must not cure too quickly. It must remain in a liquid state while it is being pumped.

Cement is pumped down the inside of the casing and then back up the annulus between the outside of the casing and the wellbore until it reaches its desired location. After the cement is in place, the Operator wants it to cure and harden as quickly as possible so that operations can continue. During this time the drilling rig is relatively idle. This period of time is recorded in drilling reports as WOC (waiting on cement). The success or failure in placing cement in the desired location in the annulus and the cement's subsequent bonding to the formation and the outside of the casing may be assessed by a cement bond log run on wireline.

## Composition of Cement

Cement contains oxides of Calcium, Aluminum, Iron, and Silicon. There are four compounds in the cement that hydrate in the presence of water to form a solid structure as the cement cures. These are tricalcium silicate ($3CaO \cdot SiO_2$), dicalcium silicate ($2CaO \cdot SiO_2$), tricalcium aluminate ($3CaO \cdot Al_2O_3$), and tetracalcium aluminoferrite ($4CaO \cdot Al_2O_3 \cdot Fe_2O_3$). The hydration process is exothermic and the existence of heat generated by curing cement can be observed if a temperature measurement device is lowered in to the well. A collection of temperatures at various depths within a well is known as a temperature log. A temperature log can be used to locate the top of cement.

## Casing Point

Once a well is drilled to its planned total depth, a decision must be made as to whether or not the well is capable of producing oil or gas in commercial quantities.

The point in time immediately after a well has been drilled to TD and before a decision has been made as to whether or not to run production casing is called the casing point. The decision must be made in a timely manner because the drilling rig will be standing by waiting on orders from the Operator at a cost of hundreds or thousands of dollars per hour.

If the well is successful and deemed to be capable of producing oil and gas, the final string of casing – the production string - must be run. Further equipment both inside the wellbore and on the surface will be installed to facilitate production. Procuring the casing and the surface facilities require substantial expenditures. So if a well does not penetrate any zones capable of paying in commercial quantities, a decision will be made to plug the well with cement and abandon it (P & A). Such a well is called a dry hole.

If all of the working interest owners agree to run casing and complete the well then each pays their share of the costs going forward as specified in the joint operating agreement. If they all agree to plug and abandon the well, then they will each pay their share of the additional cost of plugging and abandoning the well. However, if some working interest owners want to run casing and some do not, based on (a) varying points of view regarding the formation evaluation, or (b) believing that the expected returns do not justify the additional cost of running casing and attempting to produce the well, then they may elect to refuse to invest any further money. This is called "going non-consent" in most operating agreements. When this happens, the parties that want to go forward bear all further costs and share all further revenue. The parties that go non-consent are not responsible for any of the costs of running casing but they are also likely excluded from any revenue that the well produces. This depends on the details the parties agree to in their operating agreement. Let's take a closer look at how the formations that a well penetrates are evaluated for their commercial capacity to produce oil and gas.

# Chapter 5 Formation Evaluation

After a well is drilled, the next step is to evaluate the rock layers that the well has penetrated and assess their capacity to produce oil and gas in commercial quantities. A well may produce from any zone along its path, not just the target zone that the Operator had in mind when they decided to drill the well. It is from this evaluation of the formations that a decision is made as to whether or not to run casing and attempt to produce the well.

# Logging

In order to evaluate the formations that are penetrated by a new wellbore, various properties of the rocks and the fluid contained within their pores are measured. These properties include electrical, acoustic, and nuclear properties. Measurements are made using special instruments that are lowered in to the well. Measurements of these properties are usually made every three to six inches along the entire length of the wellbore from the bottom up to the top. Some measurements are made over even shorter distances. The results of all of these measurements are plotted against the depth in the well where each measurement was made. Such a plot of rock and fluid properties versus depth is called a log. And the operation wherein instruments are lowered in to a well to make these measurements is called logging. The instruments that are used to acquire the data are called logging tools.

Logging tools come in two types: wireline logging tools and logging-while-drilling tools (LWD tools).

## Electric Wireline Logging

Wireline logging tools are generally cylindrically shaped devices that are one to six inches in diameter and two to 30 feet long. They are connected end-to-end so that many different kinds of logging tools can be run in a well simultaneously. Such a string of logging tools connected end-to-end is called a logging string. A logging string is lowered in to a well on the end of a cable that is approximately one half of an inch in diameter. Inside of the cable's outer wires are seven separate electrical conductors. Each electrical conductor is a copper wire with its own insulation. These conductors are used to provide electrical power to the logging string and for digital data communication between the toolstring and the surface.

# Electric Wireline Logging Operation

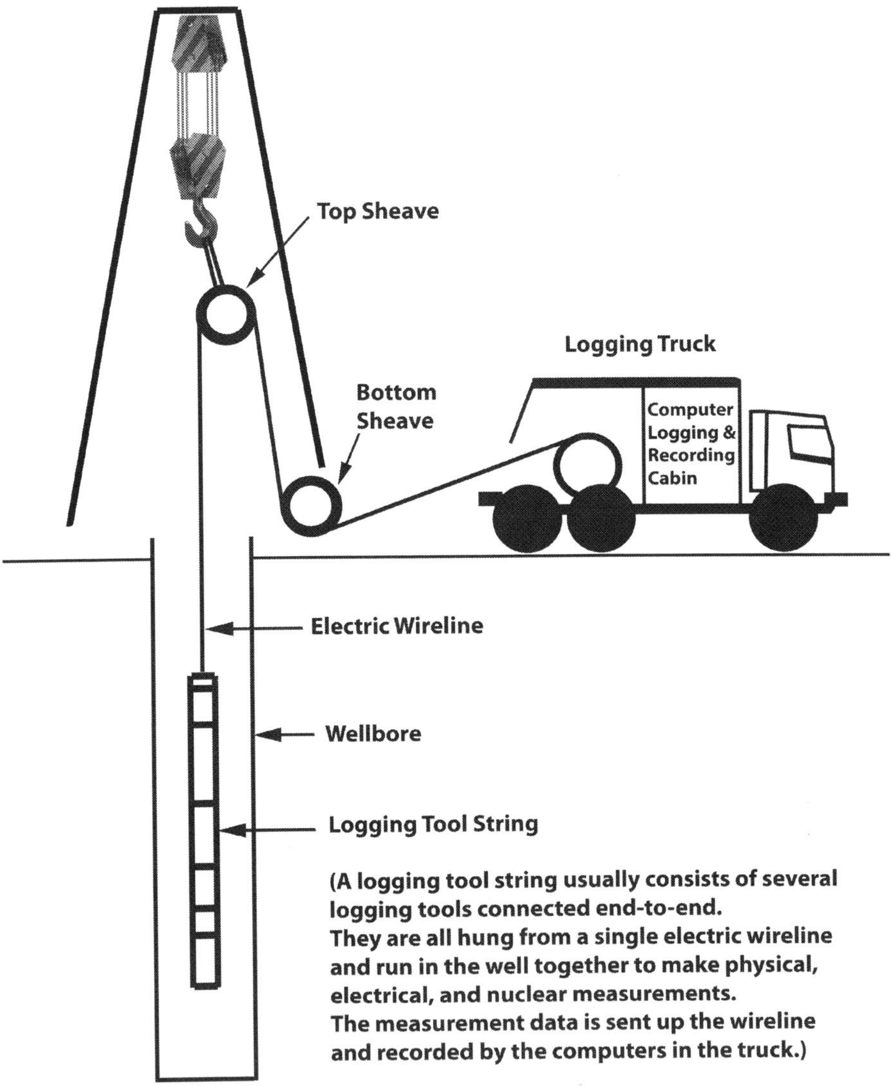


(A logging tool string usually consists of several logging tools connected end-to-end.
They are all hung from a single electric wireline and run in the well together to make physical, electrical, and nuclear measurements.
The measurement data is sent up the wireline and recorded by the computers in the truck.)

As the tools in the logging string make measurements of various electrical, acoustic, and nuclear properties of the rock, the information is sent up the electrical conductors within the wireline to a computer system at the surface that is used to record all of the data.

The cable that has the electrical conductors inside it is called electric wireline, electric line, wireline, or e-line. All of these terms are synonymous. Logging is performed by special contractors who provide the logging tools, the wireline, the computer system on the surface, and a crew of people to perform the work and produce a log.

## Logging Truck

The contractors perform the entire service from a truck known as a logging truck. The logging truck includes a motorized spool of wireline that provides the power to lower the string of logging tools in to the well and pull them back out. The logging truck also includes an air-conditioned room where the computer system is kept. In this room, the contractor's Logging Engineer operates the computer system and acquires the data while the tool string is in the hole. A member of the wireline contractor's team operates the hoist controls while lowering the tool string in to the hole and while pulling it back out. Some instruments are capable of operating while the tool is being lowered to TD; but most data is acquired while slowly pulling the tool string out of the hole. A log obtained while lowering the tools toward TD is known as a down log. The log obtained while pulling up is called the "up log".

## Logging While Drilling (LWD)

LWD stands for Logging While Drilling. These are the other kind of logging tools aside from wireline logging tools. Rather than being conveyed in to a wellbore on wireline after a wellbore has been drilled, LWD tools are placed near the bottom of a drill string between the drill bit and the drill pipe. They are part of the drill string and they measure properties of the rock and the fluids in the rock as the well is being drilled. While wireline tools have been in development since the 1930's, LWD tools did not gain strength until the 1990's. LWD tools are much larger and stronger than wireline tools because they must endure the tensions, compression, torque, and vibrations that exist in the drill string while the bit is turning and while the drill string is being run in and out of the hole. The advantage of LWD is that the data is acquired while the wellbore is being drilled so the trajectory of the well can be adjusted while the well is being drilled if necessary. LWD measurements are made very soon after the bit has penetrated the rock and are thus less influenced by subsequent drilling fluid invasion in the near wellbore region.

And because LWD tools are conveyed on heavy duty drill pipe, they can be used in hostile situations where wireline tools cannot. While not as rugged as LWD tools, wireline tools offer better data quality at a lower cost.

## Logging Tools

The rock and fluid properties that are measured by logging contractors include resistivity, porosity, natural gamma radiation, acoustic compressional wave speed, acoustic shear wave speed, magnetic resonance characteristics (similar to an MRI medical device), elemental composition, and borehole imaging.

## Resistivity Tools

Resistivity tools measure the bulk resistivity of a formation. Modern tools measure resistivity at several different radii (or depths of investigation) from the tool such as 10 inches, 20 inches, 30 inches, 60 inches, 90 inches, and 120 inches. Vertical resolution of one foot is now available. In general, high resistivity is good and low resistivity is bad. This is because oil and gas do not conduct electricity. And most rock grains do not conduct electricity although some clays in shales do conduct electricity. Saline formation water does conduct electricity. Thus pay zones that are filled with non-conductive oil and gas tend to have higher resistivities than zones that are saturated with saline formation water. Resistivity can be used in empirical equations to calculate water saturation. Measurements from various depths of investigation provide an indicator of permeability. Deeper readings are indicative of true formation resistivity while shallower readings are influenced by mud filtrate invasion if the zone is permeable.

# Gamma Ray Tools

Gamma rays are a form of high-frequency short-wavelength electromagnetic radiation emitted from the nuclei of unstable atoms. Gamma rays are continuously released in nature by certain isotopes of potassium, uranium, and thorium. One of the most common logging tools in the oil and gas industry is a gamma ray logging tool. A gamma ray tool counts the number of naturally emitted gamma rays originating from formations around the wellbore that are detected in the tool within a one-second time interval. Shales tend to contain more potassium than sandstones or carbonates. So higher gamma ray counts within a particular formation usually indicate a higher percentage of shale. Formations with low gamma ray counts are called "clean" formations and these are most likely to be non-shales such as sandstones and carbonates. Gamma ray measurements are repeated at various depth intervals within a well. They are usually made every three to six inches for the entire length of a logged interval - which can be thousands of feet. In general, a low gamma ray is good and a high gamma ray is bad because a low gamma ray is likely to be found in a non-shale such as a sandstone or a carbonate. And these are common reservoir rocks for oil and gas.

Some gamma ray tools are capable of not only counting the number of gamma rays detected at the tool but also measuring the energy level of each gamma ray. Such tools are called spectral gamma ray tools. They enable a Log Analyst to determine what elemental isotope emitted each gamma ray whether it was potassium, uranium, or thorium. Most gamma rays in most wells are emitted by potassium in shale. However, uranium and thorium sometimes appear in high concentrations. Gamma rays emitted by uranium or thorium are not related to shale content and their presence can skew an analysis if the gamma rays they emit are inadvertently assumed to be from potassium in shale. Gamma ray tools function in both open hole and cased hole. This fact allows cased hole tools such as perforating devices to be set in a well on depth with or correlated with specific zones seen on open hole logs.

## Density Porosity Tools

Porosity is commonly inferred from two nuclear measurements. The first method is called a density measurement. It employs a chemical source that emits gamma rays at a fairly constant rate in to the formation. These gamma rays collide with electrons in the formation and are deflected through an interaction called Compton's Scattering. Gamma ray detectors placed approximately 18 inches from the chemical source count the number of gamma rays received at the detector and measure the energy levels of those gamma rays.

Low-density rock has fewer electrons and thus more gamma rays will travel through the rock and be detected at the detectors. For any given grain or matrix density, lower bulk density of the rock means higher porosity.

Conversely, high-density rock has more electrons in it and thus fewer gamma rays will travel through the rock and be detected at the detectors. For a given grain or matrix density, higher bulk density of the rock means lower porosity.

Density tools are calibrated using materials of known density such as steel, magnesium, and aluminum before being run in the hole. Interpolations of log measurements between these known data points provide a quantitative measurement of the bulk density of the formation. If you know the density of the grains and the pore fluid then you can use the bulk density to calculate porosity. Sandstone is usually assumed to be 2.65 gram/cc. Limestone is assumed to be 2.71 gram/cc. And for the purpose of calculating porosity, the pore fluid density is assumed to be water with a density of 1.0 gram/cc. The elemental composition tools which will be discussed shortly can provide a more accurate grain density so that you do not need to make an assumption. The density measurement also assumes that the material has a Z/A ratio of 0.5 where Z is the atomic number and A is the atomic mass. This assumption is usually true with the notable exception of when you are logging in salt (halite).

Generally you want to find formations with high porosity because they can hold more oil and gas and they tend to have better permeability. A density tool is designed to be run decentralized. Most density tools (but not all) have a pad that is pressed against the borehole wall while logging up. This pad contains both the chemical source and the gamma ray detectors. A density tool functions only in open hole.

## Neutron Porosity Tools

The second common logging tool that measures porosity is called the neutron tool. A neutron tool uses a chemical source that emits neutrons in to the formation. These neutrons collide with hydrogen nuclei (single protons) in the formation and are slowed to thermal energy levels. The process is similar to a cue ball being slowed as it collides with other balls on a pool table. The more hydrogen there is in the formation, the sooner the neutrons are slowed to thermal levels. Once they reach thermal levels they are quickly captured by other nuclei that have an affinity for free roaming neutrons. As each neutron is captured, gamma rays are emitted from the capturing nucleus. There are detectors in the neutron tool approximately 12 inches from the source that detect and count these capture gamma rays as they are emitted. The number of neutron capture gamma rays detected at the source varies inversely with the amount of hydrogen in the formation. And most of the hydrogen in a formation is in the pore fluid - be it oil or water.

Recall that hydrogen is not a common element in the minerals that make up rock grains. So as we are measuring the hydrogen content of the formation we are effectively measuring the porosity as well. Higher hydrogen content means higher porosity. Lower hydrogen content means lower porosity.

The neutron porosity tool is calibrated in a formation of known porosity on the surface so that measurements acquired in a well can provide quantitative measurements of porosity. Neutron porosity measurements are affected by the lithology of the formation, the borehole diameter, the salinity of the water, the pore fluid, the presence or absence of gas in the pores, and the position of the tool within the wellbore. Corrections or at least considerations must be made for all of these parameters when reading a neutron log.

Most neutron tools are designed to be run decentralized. That means they are pressed against the borehole wall while logging up and acquiring data. Neutron tools can only acquire quantitative porosity measurements in open hole. They also function in cased hole but can only be used for qualitative measurement. Neutron tools can be run with other cased hole tools to provide a means of correlating cased hole logs to open hole logs.

# Acoustic Tools (Sonic Tools or Long Spaced Sonic Tools)

Acoustic tools measure the speed of compressional waves and shear waves along the borehole wall. The acoustic energy source in an acoustic tool is a piezoelectric transducer. It is a piece of ceramic that expands and contracts as voltage is applied to it. The detectors in an acoustic tool are also piezoelectric transducers. They produce voltages when compressional waves impinge on them. If the speed of compressional waves through the rock matrix and the pore fluid are known or assumed, then the measured formation speed can be used to calculate porosity. Compressional and shear wave velocities can also be used to calculate mechanical properties of the rock including Young's Modulus and Poisson's Ratio. These mechanical properties are critical to the design of hydraulic fracture stimulations.

# 3-D Resistivity for Thin Beds

A three-dimensional resistivity tool is used in formations where the Operator suspects that there may be alternating thin beds of high-resistivity sand (perhaps saturated with oil and gas) and low-resistivity shale. The low resistivity shale will fool conventional one-dimensional resistivity tools and cause the whole formation to seem to have a low resistivity and thus appear to be 100% saturated with water. But a three dimensional resistivity tool can see thin layers of oil-saturated sandstone in between layers of low-resistivity shale.

The output products of a three-dimensional resistivity log are Resistivity of the Sand, Resistivity of the Shale, Shale Volume, and Sand Volume. All of these outputs can be reached regardless of how thin the beds may be.

# Magnetic Resonance Tools

Magnetic Resonance tools use the same principle as MRI medical imaging devices. They use a strong permanent magnet and a controlled alternating magnetic field to tip the protons of hydrogen nuclei in the pore fluids within a formation back and forth. Protons within the pore fluid in the formation are charged particles having a mass and thus are essentially tiny magnets themselves. As they move back and forth in response to the applied magnetic fields they emit radio waves that are received by a detector in the tool. From those detected radio waves we can determine the porosity of the formation and the relative distribution of the porosity with respect to grain sizes. You learn not only the porosity but also how much of it is bound and how much is moveable. Magnetic resonance tools can also be used for fluid identification. You can determine if a zone contains oil, water, or gas. A magnetic resonance tool functions only in open hole.

## Elemental Composition Tools

In recent years the technology has been developed to determine the fractions of Silicon, Calcium, Iron, Aluminum, Sulfur, Magnesium, Carbon, Titanium, Potassium, Uranium, and Thorium within the rock matrix. Knowing the relative quantities of these elements within a formation allows you to determine the mineral content and clay content of the formation.

## Borehole Imaging Tools

You can also create images of the borehole wall using specialized high-resolution acoustic and resistivity measurements. The acoustic method is similar to a medical ultrasound device. The images provide fine definition of bed boundaries and fractures.

# Fluid Sampling

In addition to measuring the properties of the rock, logging contractors are also capable of extracting fluid samples from formations they see on logs. They can extract both liquids and gases and bring them to the surface. Multiple fluid samples can be acquired during each trip in to the well. If a chamber of oil is extracted from a formation and brought to the surface, it gives the Operator and any other working interest owners high confidence that their log analysis was correct and a particular rock formation does indeed contain oil. Complex systems within the tool compress the fluid to keep it in single phase (100% liquid or 100% gas) as it is brought to the surface. Single phase samples yield more accurate compositional measurements in the laboratory than do samples that arrive at the laboratory in two phases (part oil and part gas).

## Pressure Tests

The same instruments that are used to extract fluid samples can be used to measure the reservoir pressures of formations seen on open hole logs. Pressure measurements can be used to determine if a reservoir is at virgin pressure or if two zones are in pressure communication. A series of pressures at several depths can establish a pressure gradient and thus identify the fluid within the zone based on its apparent density.

## Coring

Perhaps the best method of analyzing a formation is to bring a sample of the formation to the surface so that we can look at it, touch it, feel it, and test it. This is called coring. Cores are samples of rock taken from known formations in a well. There are three ways to obtain cores: whole cores, rotary sidewall cores and percussion sidewall cores.

## Whole Cores

The first and best method is to take a "whole core" while drilling a well. To accomplish this, a special drill bit known as a core bit is placed at the bottom of the drill string in lieu of a standard bit. A core bit is shaped like a donut. It has a hole in its center. As the core bit drills, a portion of the formation passes untouched through the donut hole in the middle of the bit and up in to the inside of the drill string. A special retainer is placed above the drill bit to receive the core. When the desired length of core has been drilled, the drill string is pulled out of the hole with the core retained inside of it. Cores obtained in this way are tens to hundreds of feet in length. They give Geologists and Petrophysicists the best possible understanding of the formation penetrated by the well. Cores are analyzed in a laboratory to measure rock and fluid properties. Although obtaining a whole core provides the best formation evaluation it is only performed in a small percentage of drilling operations because of its high cost.

Note: The Bureau of Economic Geology's climate-controlled Houston Research Center stores over 900,000 boxes of cores and cuttings. Adding their facilities in Austin and Midland brings the total to over 2 million boxes of geologic material. The facilities are open to the public.

Visit http://www.beg.utexas.edu/

## Rotary Sidewall Cores

The second kind of core is a rotary sidewall core. Wireline logging contractors have special tools with drill bits that are one to three inches in diameter. These tools, called rotary coring tools, can be conveyed on wireline to a desired depth in a well. The drill bit is shaped like a donut. It rotates and drills a small core from the side of the borehole wall. Rotary cores are one to four inches long and one to three inches in diameter. Tens of rotary cores can be extracted within a few hours. These cores are of very high quality and can be used reliably for laboratory measurements.

## Percussion Sidewall Cores

The third method of obtaining cores is called percussion sidewall coring. In this method a small heavy-duty metal cup about the size of a medicine glass is conveyed in to a well on wireline. When it reaches the depth where a rock sample is desired, the cup is forced in to a rock formation using high-pressure expanding gas. A sample of the rock becomes lodged in the cup and the cup becomes temporarily stuck in the formation. Cables attached to the cup are used to pull it out of the formation while the core sample remains in the cup. Logging contractors are capable of obtaining 25 to 150 sidewall core samples during a single trip in to a well. So when the sidewall coring tool is brought back to the surface it contains 25 to 150 core samples from various depths. The cups, known as core barrels, are each placed under a special hand press and pushed out of the metal core barrels. When pressed out of the metal core barrel, each core sample falls in to a separate clear glass jar. A lid is immediately placed on each jar and tightened so that any natural gas that escapes from the core will be detected when the cores are analyzed in the lab.

Sidewall cores are usually analyzed within hours of being recovered. Although they are unsuitable for permeability measurements, they are a superb means of quickly identifying the lithology and the fluid content of a formation at a very low cost. Cores that contain oil are often obvious upon visual inspection. A core can be placed under a black light and any oil in the core will fluoresce (appear fluorescent yellow). Cores that contain water are often equally obvious – looking much like a wet rock lifted from a bucket of water. Natural gas can be detected in a laboratory using a sniffer. The device is similar to a hypodermic needle. It is pushed through the lid of the glass jar that holds the core. The device sniffs the air inside the jar to detect the presence of methane and other hydrocarbon gases that have escaped from the core sample.

## Final Formation Evaluation

All of the logs, fluid data, and core data are considered in totality to perform the final formation evaluation at the casing point. A decision must be made to either deem a well to be commercial and run casing or to deem the well to be a dry hole and simply plug the well with cement and abandon it.

The science of analyzing all of the log, fluid, and core measurements and determining what they mean is called Petrophysics.

To learn more about the Petrophysicists and Log Analysts who perform this kind of work, visit the Society of Petrophysicists and Well Log Analysts at www.spwla.org.

If a well is a dry hole, production casing will not be run. The state oil and gas regulatory agency will be contacted and instructions will be provided to the Operator as to where to place cement plugs in the wellbore. The Operator will place cement plugs in the wellbore at the prescribed depths and then cut the casing at least three feet below ground level and weld a metal cap to seal the well. But if a well is successful then the next steps are to run production casing, complete the well, and begin production.

# Chapter 6 Completion

Everything that is done in a well after the production casing is run and prior to initiating production is called the completion. After the production casing is run and cemented in place, and the wellhead is secured to the top of the well, the well is stable. It is not going to collapse because it has casing from the bottom all the way to the surface. And it is not going to blow out because it has casing, cement outside the casing, fluid inside the well called completion fluid, and a wellhead that is closed. A typical completion fluid is 2%

KCl water.

Because the well is in a stable condition, the drilling rig can be rigged down and moved off of location. The invoices for the drilling contractor, the casing providers, the cementers, the logging contractor, and several smaller providers can be paid. Their work is done.

At this point we have invested a large amount of capital. We have a well on our lease that we know is capable of producing oil and gas but it is not yet producing. Completing the well is the final series of steps before production begins. The time between the end of the drilling operation and the commencement of the completion can be hours to months depending on the Operator and the availability of the next group of suppliers and contractors.

# Perforating

The next step is to create holes in the casing at the depth where the oil or gas zone is located. This is accomplished by lowering a perforating device in to the well on wireline or on tubing. Tubing is small-diameter metal pipe that fits inside the production casing. The perforating device is set to create holes in the production casing and the cement that is surrounding the outside of the casing. The holes created by the perforating device will often extend through the casing, through the cement, and up to 48 inches in to the rock formation that is saturated with oil and or natural gas. The perforating device is then removed from the well and a small amount of completion fluid in the wellbore may be removed by a method known as swabbing so that the pressure in the wellbore is somewhat less than the pressure in the formation. This allows the fluid in the formation to enter the wellbore and begin flowing to the surface.

Perforating devices vary widely. An Engineer can model the performance of various perforating devices and recommend one that is best suited for a particular casing size and thickness, the cement strength, and the formation's lithology, porosity, and compressional stress.

After perforating the well and swabbing some of the fluid in the wellbore, the oil or gas will begin to flow in to the wellbore and up toward the surface. The flow rate is controlled by a series of chokes and valves at the top of the well called the wellhead.

## Hydraulic Fracture Stimulation

The flow rate of the well may be enhanced by several means of stimulation. The first is hydraulic fracturing. This method has been in use for decades. A liquid such as water or a gas such as nitrogen is pumped down the wellbore to the perforations. The fluid, whether liquid or gas, exerts a stress on the formation and causes it to crack or fracture. Pumping of the fracture fluid continues and the fracture propagates further and further from the well bore. Finally the pressure on the fracturing fluid is released and the formation closes on the fracture. However, before it closes, sand, beads, or similar materials, known as proppants, are placed in the fracture space so that the fracture remains propped open slightly even after the fracture fluid pressure is release. The propped fracture will have a relatively high permeability and it will extend tens to hundreds of feet from the wellbore. The amount of proppant that is pumped can vary from a few thousand pounds in a small job to hundreds of thousands of pounds in a large frac job. Once the fracture is created and held open by the proppant, fluids that are at great distances from the wellbore will readily flow in to the fracture and they will do so much sooner than they would otherwise flow to the wellbore. Upon entering the propped open fracture, the oil and gas flows around the proppant and follows the path of the fracture to the wellbore where they then flow to the surface. A hydraulic fracture treatment is intended to increase the production rate of a well. Knowledge of fluid mechanics and rock mechanics are necessary to design a successful hydraulic fracture treatment (also known as a frac job).

## Acidizing

A second method of stimulating a well is acidizing. Under this method, a strong acid is pumped down the well bore and out through the perforations. The acid will react with limestone in the region around the borehole and can open path ways for oil to flow from the limestone formation to the perforations.

## Production Test

After a well has been perforated and any planned stimulation is performed, the well can be tested to determine its productive capacity. The data gathered during a production test is submitted to the state oil and gas regulatory agency.

## Multiple Completions

A well may have penetrated several zones that are capable of producing oil and gas. An Operator may produce one at a time or may elect to produce multiple zones simultaneously. The simplest method is to begin with the deepest zone first. Test it. Produce it. Plug it. Move up the hole and repeat the process with the next zone. It can take years to deplete each zone one-by-one in series. A slightly more difficult method is to produce the best zone first - even if it is not the deepest zone. This can be done but it adds cost and risk to the workovers that will be required to plug the first zone and move downhole to the next zone. Moving further along the cost and complexity scale, it is possible to produce multiple zones simultaneously. It is not simple; it is not cheap; and it requires consent of the state oil and gas regulatory agency. However, it can be done where economics justify it.

# Chapter 7 Production

## Artificial Lift

If the reservoir pressure is high enough, it will push the fluids all the way to the surface and establish a flowing well. If the reservoir pressure is capable of pushing the fluids some distance up the well but not all the way to the surface, then the well is not a flowing well. In the case of a well that does not have sufficient pressure to push the fluid to surface, a means of lifting the fluids out of the hole must be employed. There are several different kinds of artificial lift.

# Rod Pumping (Sucker Rod Lift)

The most well-known and easily recognized form of artificial lift is sucker rod lift. It employs the familiar pump jack or rocking horse to lift a long string of metal rods up and down inside the tubing of an oil well. First a string of tubing that is 2-3/8 or 2-7/8 inches in outside diameter is run in the well from the surface to the reservoir. The bottom of the tubing is anchored in place against the casing and the top of the tubing is hung in tension

**A pump jack. The up and down motion of the horse's head raises and lowers a string of sucker rods which actuates a pump at the bottom of the well and pushes oil to the surface.**

**A tank battery and a pump jack. The fiberglass tank on the far left is the water tank. The two steel tanks in the center and on the right side are oil stock tanks. The pump jack is at the far right side of the photograph.**

in the wellhead. Then a long string of solid metal or fiberglass rods known as sucker rods are run inside the tubing and attached to a pump at the bottom of the well. The pump may be on the end of the rod string or it may be on the bottom of the tubing. As the pump jack's head moves up and down, the long string of sucker rods moves up and down. The action of the rods moving up and down powers the pump (similar to a bicycle pump) which pumps the oil up the inside of the tubing to the surface. The rods and the oil are both inside the tubing. The rods are small enough that there is plenty of room for both the oil and the sucker rods inside the tubing.

## Submersible Pump

Another form of artificial lift is a submersible pump. Under this method an electric pump is placed in the bottom of the well at the end of a string of tubing. An electrical cable on the outside of the tubing provides electric power from the surface to the pump. The pump runs continuously and pumps fluid up the inside of the tubing to the surface. This can continue uninterrupted for years at a time. Submersible pumps are used when high pump rates are required.

## Gas Lift

A third form of artificial lift is gas lift. Here, compressed gas is pushed down the space between the inside of the casing and the outside of the tubing (the tubing-casing annulus), though a special group of valves in the tubing near the bottom of the tubing string, and then up the inside of the tubing to the surface. As the gas bubbles through the oil inside the tubing it reduces the hydrostatic pressure inside the tubing. The reduction in pressure inside the tubing is sufficient to allow the fluid in the wellbore to flow to the surface.

## Surface Facilities

In addition to any artificial lift equipment that is in the well; a few pieces of surface equipment are also required.

First a pipe made of steel, plastic or fiber glass will be installed which will carry the produced oil and gas a short distance from the well to the separation, treatment, and storage facilities.

# Gun Barrel and Stock Tanks

**A gun barrel and three oil stock tanks. The water tank is not shown in this picture.**

Oil will first enter a tall tank called a gun barrel or a free water knock out. While in the gun barrel the oil naturally migrates to the top because it is less dense than water. Water moves to the bottom. Oil then passes out of the gun barrel to oil stock tanks where it is stored until a truck arrives to haul it away. Oil stock tanks are usually constructed of steel and have capacities of several hundred barrels each. Water passes out the bottom of the gun barrel in to the water tanks. Water tanks are usually constructed of fiberglass.

**A water truck loads produced water from the fiberglass water tank at the far right.**

*Safety Tip:*
*When visiting your oil tanks, stay on the catwalk beside the tanks. Never walk on the top of an oil stock tank. If the roof collapses and you fall inside you will not float on the oil and their will not be any oxygen in the tank for you to breathe.*

## Dehydrators

If a gas stream contain hydrates it may first pass through a dehydrator where glycols are added. A dehydrator removes water from gas and prevents the formation of hydrates. A hydrate is a methane molecule surrounded by water molecules. Hydrates looks like ice or snow and can clog flowlines.

## Separators

Most wells produce a combination of liquid hydrocarbons, gaseous hydrocarbons, and liquid water at the surface. Separators are used to separate these three phases. Oil goes to a stock tank where it awaits transport by pipeline or truck. Water goes to a water tank where it awaits removal by a truck or is piped to a disposal well. And gas is connected to and sold in to a gas gathering system.

Hydrocarbons are most valuable in the liquid phase. So whenever possible, ethane, propane, and butane are retained in the liquid form. An Operator may use a single separator or a series of separators operating at successively lower pressures to retain as many of these molecules as possible in the liquid phase.

Separators are rated by their operating pressures. They come in two types: two-phase and three-phase.
A two-phase separator separate liquids from gas. The liquid that exits a two-phase separator may contain both oil and water. A three-phase separator separates oil, water, and gas in to three separate flow lines.

# Sale of Produced Oil & Gas

## Selling Crude Oil

Almost every crude oil has commercial value. It can be sold to a refiner or to a marketing company who will ultimately sell it to a refinery. There is not one price for crude oil as one might believe after hearing the price of oil quoted on the financial news. That price quote is for the near month futures

**A crude oil transport truck hauls crude oil that it has just loaded from an independent oil company's oil stock tank on a lease in Texas.**

contract price of a barrel of oil defined in the contract with a specific composition to be delivered to a specific location by a specific date. In reality, there are many different kinds of crude oils with many different compositions being produced at thousands of well sites around the world that will be delivered to numerous destinations around the world by various transportation methods on every day of the year. Transportation methods for oil include trucks, pipelines, ships, and trains.

**A crude oil tanker has just off-loaded its crude oil in to the large white storage tanks on the left side of the picture. A few crude oil tanker train cars are visible at the far left.**

The actual price received for a particular barrel of crude oil depends on its current location, molecular composition, the projected cost of refining it, the cost to transport it to a refinery, and to some extent the seller's market knowledge and negotiating skills. The near month futures price as reported in the financial news often serves as a reference point for negotiations but your actual price received will be higher or lower.

**Crude oil tanker cars in front of a storage tank at a refinery.**

## Selling Natural Gas

Natural gas is sold from the well site in to a network of pipelines that transport the gas to processing plants or end-users. Like crude oil, natural gas comes out of the ground in many different compositions. Its commercial value depends on its energy content (sometimes called Btu content), its location, the cost of transporting it, and the marketing and negotiating skills of the seller.

**A gas pipeline marker at a road crossing.**

The available gas transporters in an area can be identified before a well is drilled. Near any given well site there may be zero, one, or several gas gathering companies available. All gatherers and purchasers are registered with the state regulatory agency. They can also be found by simply observing gas pipeline markers in the area. Each pipeline company will have pipelines in a unique location with a unique line pressure. In all cases a connecting pipeline must be laid from the lease to the pipeline company's pipeline. If a connecting pipeline must be laid across the land of a third party land owner, then an easement must be obtained - often for a flat fee or a fixed priced for each cubic foot of gas that is transported across the third party's property.

An Operator may receive several different offers from the gas gathering companies an area. Gathering companies that are further from the well site may offer a better price as an incentive for the Operator to make the investment required to lay a longer connecting pipeline. The purchasing pipeline company may request a nominal fee to cover the costs of making a connection to their pipeline. It is best if an agreement is reached regarding the purchase price of any gas before the well is drilled.

# Sales Pipeline Pressure

The pressure in the pipeline you will be selling gas in to is critical. The pressure in the Operator's flowline must be greater than the pressure in the purchaser's pipeline. If not, the gas from the well will not flow in to the purchaser's pipeline and no sale can be made. Most new gas wells have sufficient pressure to push gas in to a purchaser's gathering system. But as the reservoir pressure declines, there may be a time in the future when a gas compressor must be used to boost the pressure of the gas from the wellhead to the pressure of the purchaser's pipeline. If using a compressor is not feasible then the economic limit of the well will be reached when the wellhead pressure equals the purchaser's line pressure.

**Pressure Gauge**

# Chapter 8 Reservoir Drive Mechanisms

There are several drive mechanisms in oil and gas reservoirs that push oil and natural gas toward a wellbore. The drive mechanism and the reservoir pressure together determine the rate that oil and gas will be produced over time. This is important because it affects your revenue over time.

## Water Drive Oil Reservoir

In a Water Drive Oil Reservoir, there is

a large aquifer of formation water below the oil reservoir. It pushes against the oil and displaces it like a piston as oil is produced. If the perforations are only in the oil zone and completely above the water, the initial production may be at or near 100% oil.

Over time the oil-water contact will rise and some of the water will begin to finger through the inhomogeneities in the oil zone where the relative permeability of water is higher. Eventually some of this water will break-through to the perforations. Formation water will be produced along with the oil. From that point forward, the production will include both oil and water and the oil cut will gradually decline over time. However, the reservoir pressure may not decline significantly because water from below replaces the oil and water that have been produced.

The annual production rate of the oil

will then decline exponentially over time. Roughly 80% of all wells have a production decline rate that is between 12% and 30%. A 12% decline rate means that each year a well produces 88% of the amount of oil that it produced in the preceding year. A 30% decline rate means that each year a well produces 70% of the amount of oil that it produced in the preceding year. All other things being equal, an oil reservoir with a water-drive mechanism will have a lower (better) decline rate and a higher ultimate recovery than an equivalent reservoir with a different drive mechanism. Water-drive is the best way to produce oil.

## Solution Gas Drive Oil Reservoir

In a solution gas drive reservoir, there is hydrocarbon gas dissolved inside the liquid oil. As oil is produced the pressure of the reservoir will eventually decline to the bubble point pressure for that oil and some of the dissolved gas will come out of solution and assume a gaseous phase. These small bubbles of gas push against the oil and push it toward the wellbore. Both oil and gas will be produced from the well. As the gas is produced the reservoir pressure falls. As the reservoir pressure falls lower and lower more and more gas will come out of solution and the gas-oil ratio will increase with time. Eventually the oil driving process will fail because it will require more gas than is coming out of solution. The reservoir pressure will finally fall.

With all other things being equal a solution gas drive oil reservoir will have a lower ultimate recovery than a water drive oil reservoir. Some Operators of large solution gas drive oil fields find ways to re-inject their produced gas and even add nitrogen to it as a means of maintaining a high reservoir pressure.

# Gas Cap Drive Oil Reservoir

In a gas cap drive oil reservoir, there is large gas reservoir immediately above the oil reservoir. The pressure of the gas is exerted down against the oil. The pressure from the gas above the oil pressurizes the oil to equal the gas's pressure at the gas-oil interface. When the wellbore is perforated in the oil zone, the gas in the gas cap begins to push the oil down toward the perforations. If the wellbore perforations are only in the oil zone and completely below the gas cap, the initial production may at or near 100% oil. If the pressure at the perforations is low enough, some of the gas will begin to form a cone of gas from the gas cap down to the perforations. Eventually some of this gas will "break-through" and be seen in the produced fluid along with the oil. From that point forward, the production will include both oil and gas. This is an undesirable circumstance because the production of gas from the gas cap will cause the pressure in the gas cap to decline and thus exert less pressure on the oil reservoir. As less pressure is exerted on the oil reservoir, the oil production rate decreases and the amount of oil that can ultimately be recovered is lessened.

So when an Operator knows that an oil reservoir's drive mechanism is a gas cap, the Operator will seek to perforate the wells only in the oil zone and as far as possible below the gas so that gas from the gas cap is not produced and thus the pressure in the gas cap is kept as high as possible for as long as possible while oil is being produced. After the oil reservoir has been depleted the gas cap can be perforated and produced.

## Volumetric Gas Reservoir

In a volumetric gas reservoir, gas exists by itself within the pores of the rock essentially without any oil or water at the reservoir boundaries and within a relatively fixed volume. The pressure of the gas simply declines as the gas is produced. Producing a volumetric gas reservoir (also known as a depletion drive gas reservoir) is similar to opening the valve on a scuba diver's air tank and allowing the air to blow out.

A volumetric reservoir has the best drive mechanism for producing natual gas. It provides the highest ultimate recovery.

## Water Drive Gas Reservoir

In a water-drive gas reservoir, there is a large water reservoir below the gas reservoir and it pushes against the gas and displaces the gas like a piston as the gas is produced. If the wellbore perforations are only in the gas zone and completely above the water, the initial production may at or near 100% gas. Because the water moves up and displaces gas as the gas is produced, the gas reservoir's pressure does not decline as much as it would if the water were not present. If the well is sufficiently choked at the surface, the reservoir pressure and the gas flow rate will be nearly constant over time. From the Operator's viewpoint, the well will seem as if it will produce at a constant rate indefinitely. This characteristic can make the well appear to be an attractive purchase. Who wouldn't want to purchase an income stream that will last forever? However, as soon as the water that is displacing the gas from below reaches the perforations, the gas production will suddenly cease. And the only fluid the well will produce is water.

Some Operators produce water drive gas reservoirs at very high rates in the hope that they can produce gas from locations in the reservoir that are both above and below the perforations. Others choose to produce these reservoirs at very slow rates so as to minimize the pressure differential between the water and the perforations and thus minimize the odds of "coning" water up to the perforations from the water below. The downside of this method is that any gas that is in the reservoir but above the depth of the perforations will not be produced and will be left in the reservoir when the water reaches the perforations. Water drive gas reservoirs have a relatively constant flowing tubing pressure and flow rate until the day when the water reaches the perforations and all gas production suddenly ceases.

# Chapter 9
# Workovers

From time to time it may be necessary to make mechanical changes within a well. The need may stem from the reservoir or from the mechanical equipment in the well. When one pay zone is depleted, or the water production has increased beyond manageable levels, the Operator may plug back that zone and recomplete the well in another pay zone at a shallower depth. Mechanical problems within the wellbore are also encountered because all downhole equipment is subject to constant wear, abrasion, and corrosion.

Down hole pumps fail. Holes develop in tubing. Valves leak. And sucker rods part.

Recompletions to new pay zones and the repair of mechanical problems are performed by working over a well using a workover rig. A workover rig is similar to a drilling rig in that it has a derrick and a hoisting system. But workover rigs are usually smaller than drilling rigs because they only need to hoist tubing and sucker rods which weigh much less than drill pipe.

While not trivial, the day rates for workover rigs are considerably less than drilling rigs. Drilling wells on land costs hundreds of thousands to millions of dollars depending on the depth and complexity. In comparison, working over wells on land typically costs tens of thousands to hundreds of thousands of dollars depending on depth and complexity.

**A workover rig.**

# Chapter 10 Plugging and Abandoning a Well

Over time a well's production rate will decline. Eventually the income from the sale of produced oil and gas will equal the operating expenses of the well. This is the economic limit for a well. If production continues beyond the economic limit, the costs of operating the well will exceed the revenue. It is at this time that the producing zone must be plugged. If there are other reserves behind pipe, the Operator will recomplete the well and begin producing from the next zone.

If there are no reserves behind pipe, the well must be plugged and abandoned (P & A). The Operator will contact the state oil and gas regulatory agency and inform them that the well will be plugged and abandoned. The state oil and gas regulatory agency will provide the Operator with depths where cement plugs must be placed within the well. The Operator will then remove any downhole equipment and possibly some of the casing from the well if it is economically feasible. Next, cement plugs are placed at the depths required by the state oil and gas regulatory agency. Finally, the top of the casing is cut several feet below ground level and a steel cap is welded on top of it. The purpose of the cement plugs is to prevent fluids from migrating up or down inside the wellbore and to prevent the possibility of contamination of shallow fresh water zones from deeper hydrocarbon zones. Lastly, the surface facilities are removed. If the oil and gas lease is in its secondary term and there is no other production on the lease, then the oil and gas lease will terminate because of a lack of production in paying quantities.

A similar plugging procedure is used when a dry hole is drilled. The difference is that when a dry hole is drilled there is no downhole equipment to remove and there are no surface facilities to remove.

Hopefully all parties involved have enjoyed great financial benefit by this time and a new well can be drilled in a new location and the entire cycle can begin again. Oil and gas investors earn returns; mineral interest owners receive royalties; hundreds of oilfield supplier and contractor jobs are supported; state, local, and federal governments receive substantial tax revenues; and the United

States of America receives the energy it needs to power its economy and provide prosperity and security for its people. God bless the oil industry and God bless America.

# Part II
# Oil and Gas Business

# Chapter 11
# Oil and Gas Leases

Before drilling a well, we must acquire the rights to drill for and produce oil and natural gas on a tract of land. The necessary document is an oil and gas lease. An oil and gas lease is a written contract wherein a mineral interest owner, known as the Lessor, grants the right to explore for oil, natural gas, and other hydrocarbons to an oil company or other entity, known as the Lessee, for a specific period of time. Before we discuss how mineral interests are conveyed, let's discuss what a mineral interest is.

## Mineral Interest

A mineral interest in oil and gas is the right to search for, develop, and produce oil and gas on a tract of land and the right to possess oil and gas in place under a property. In most nations of the world, the government owns all of the mineral rights. However, the United States is an exception. In the U.S. most of the mineral rights are privately owned, although the federal and state governments do own a substantial portion of the total mineral rights because they own the mineral rights under federal and state lands.

Private ownership of mineral rights provides an extraordinary opportunity for small U.S. companies and private investors to explore for oil and gas in the United States!

## Mineral Interest Implied Easement

Ownership of the mineral interest in a parcel of land includes not only ownership of the minerals but also an implied easement to use the surface as is reasonably necessary to extract the minerals. Without this implied easement, a mineral interest would be worthless.

## Mineral Interest Incidents

In addition to the right to search for, develop, and produce oil and gas, a mineral interest also includes the following four incidents:

1. The right to receive profits from and the obligation to pay costs incurred in a search to develop minerals.

2. The right to sell the mineral interest.

3. The right to lease a mineral interest to another person or entity through an

oil and gas lease. The right to lease is referred to as the executive right when it is severed from the rest of the mineral interest.

4. The right to benefits provided under the terms of an oil and gas lease. These benefits include a royalty, delay rentals, shut-in royalty payments, and a lease bonus.

Land men and attorneys often work together to secure oil and gas leases from mineral interest owners for their clients. The website for the American Association of Petroleum Land Men is www.landman.org.

## Surface Interest

The surface interest is all other interests in a property that are not included in the mineral interest. The surface interest is encumbered by and servient to the mineral interest.

## Sovereignty

In the beginning, all land was owned by the government. This time period is known as sovereignty. Individual land ownership in the United States began when governments first granted lands to private citizens. Ownership was passed forward from one person to another by deed, by inheritance, or by other conveyance through the present day.

## Severability

The original ownership after sovereignty included both surface rights and mineral interests. Many land tracts today are owned by an individual who still retains both the surface rights and the mineral interests. However, surface rights and mineral rights are severable. That means that they can be conveyed separately. The result is that one person or entity may own the surface interest in a tract of land while another person or entity may own the mineral interest.

## Leasehold Interest

A leasehold interest is the right to the mineral interest that is conveyed by a Lessor to a Lessee through an oil and gas lease. A leasehold interest is also called a working interest. This is the interest that is possessed by an oil company that has leased a property for oil and gas exploration.

## Royalty Interest

A royalty interest is a share of the revenue received from production. A land owner's royalty or Lessor's royalty is the share of production revenue set out in the royalty clause of an oil and gas lease. If a successful well is drilled, this royalty represents the bulk of the financial reward the mineral interest owner will receive in return for leasing their mineral interest to a Lessee. Royalty interest owners do not have any surface use rights that stem from their royalty interest.

## Overriding Royalty Interest

An overriding royalty is a royalty granted by a leasehold interest owner by filing a simple assignment of such in the public records. Overriding royalties are usually granted as compensation to Geologists, Geophysicists, Land Men, Attorneys, Investment Sponsors and others who contribute time and professional services to a drilling venture. An overriding royalty terminates when the underlying oil and gas lease terminates.

## Oil and Gas Lease

An oil and gas lease is a written contract wherein a mineral interest owner, known as the Lessor, grants the right to explore for oil, natural gas, and other hydrocarbons for a specific period of time to an oil company or other entity, known as the Lessee. An oil and gas lease is both a conveyance and a contract. It conveys certain mineral rights and establishes conditions which the Lessee must meet during the term of the lease. An oil and gas lease is considered a "Deed with the Possibility of Reverter" which means the interest may revert to the Lessor when the lease expires.

# Enforceability of a Contract

A contract is a legally enforceable promise between two or more parties to do or not to do a particular thing.

Certain items must be present to create a contract:

1. An offer.
2. Acceptance of the offer without qualification.
3. Sufficient consideration.
4. Legal subject matter.
5. Competent parties.
6. Intent of the parties to enter into a contract.

An oil and gas lease need only be signed by the Lessor. Recording of the oil and gas lease in the county courthouse by the Lessee implies acceptance of the Lease by the Lessee.

# Case Law and Modern Lease Language

Oil and gas leases have existed for decades. When the industry was in its infancy, oil and gas leases were simpler and often silent on many key points. But in the fullness of time, numerous civil cases have been adjudicated to yield an abundance of case law. Modern oil and gas leases are written with the advantage of having decades of industry activity and thousands of pages of oil and gas case law. So modern oil and gas leases have language that covers most of the eventualities that are encountered.

# Key Clauses in Oil and Gas Leases

The following are key clauses that are included in most oil and gas leases:

# Granting Clause

The granting clause of an oil and gas lease describes the land area that is covered by the lease, what substances are covered by the lease - such as oil and gas and other minerals, and what rights are being acquired by the Lessee. The term "gas" may also be further defined to include or not include any gaseous substance - not just hydrocarbon gases. For example, helium is a valuable product that may be produced. It is a gaseous substance but it is not a hydrocarbon so clarity is required.

# Example Granting Clause

In consideration of a cash bonus in hand paid and the covenants herein contained, Lessor hereby grants, leases and lets exclusively to Lessee the following described land, hereinafter called leased premises:

(Legal Description Inserted Here)

in the County of _____________, State of , containing ____ gross acres, more or less (including any interests therein which Lessor may hereafter acquire by reversion, prescription or otherwise), for the purpose of exploring for, developing, producing and marketing oil and gas, along with all hydrocarbon and nonhydrocarbon substances produced in association therewith ("Oil and Gas Substances"). The term "gas" as used herein includes helium, carbon dioxide, gaseous sulfur compounds, methane produced from coal formations and other commercial gases, as well as normal hydrocarbon gases.

## Mother Hubbard Clause

A "Mother Hubbard" clause of an oil and gas lease is often included in the granting clause. It acts to include all land owned by the Lessor, if any, that are adjacent to and contiguous with the land in the legal description so that the lease covers all land owned by the Lessor in that location, regardless of whether the legal description perfectly describes the boundaries of the land. In this way, no small slivers of land are inadvertently left out of the lease.

## Example Mother Hubbard Clause

In addition to the above-described land, this lease and the term "leased premises" also covers accretions and any small strips or parcels of land now or hereafter owned by Lessor which are contiguous or adjacent to the above-described land, and, in consideration of the aforementioned cash bonus, Lessor agrees to execute at Lessee's request any additional or supplemental instruments for a more complete or accurate description of the land so covered.

# In Gross Provision

An In Gross provision in an oil and gas lease is also often included in the granting clause to establish the number of acres that a lease will be assumed to contain, regardless of whether it contains slightly more or less, so that payments in the lease that are based on the number of acres can be made with certainty even when the exact acreage of a lease may be unknown or later found to be slightly higher or lower than it was believed to be at the time a lease was signed.

# Example In Gross Provision

For the purpose of determining the amount of any payments based on acreage hereunder, the number of gross acres above specified shall be deemed correct, whether actually more or less.

# Term Clause (Also known as the Habendum Clause)

The term clause of an oil and gas lease, also known as the habendum clause, defines the duration of the lease. This is usually divided in to two parts: the primary term and the extended term. The primary term is essentially the amount of time that a Lessee has to drill the first well. Simply speaking, if the drilling of a well is not begun during the primary term, the lease expires. If at least one well is drilled during the primary term, then the extended term defines the amount of time that the lease will remain in effect -- usually for as long as a well produces in paying quantities.

# Example Term Clause or Habendum Clause

This lease shall be in force for a primary term of 3 years from the date hereof, and for as long thereafter as oil or gas or other substances covered hereby are produced in paying quantities from the leased premises or from lands pooled or unitized therewith or this lease is otherwise maintained in effect pursuant to the provisions hereof.

## Dry Hole & Cessation of Production Clauses

The dry hole and cessation of production clauses in an oil and gas lease describe how a lease will be maintained in the event that a dry hole is drilled or all production from an existing well ceases.

## Example Dry Hole & Cessation of Production Clauses

If Lessee drills a well which is incapable of producing in paying quantities (hereinafter called "dry hole") on the leased premises or lands pooled or unitized therewith, or if all production (whether or not in paying quantities) permanently ceases from any cause, including a revision of unit boundaries pursuant to the provisions of this lease or the action of any governmental authority, then in the event this lease is not otherwise being maintained in force it shall nevertheless remain in force if Lessee commences further operations for reworking an existing well or for drilling an additional well or for otherwise obtaining or restoring production on the leased premises or lands pooled or unitized therewith within 90 days after completion of operations on such dry hole or within 90 days after such cessation of all production. If after the primary term this lease is not otherwise being maintained in force, but Lessee is then engaged in Operations, as defined below, this lease shall remain in force so long as any one or more of such Operations are prosecuted with no interruption of more than 90 consecutive days, and if any such Operations result in the production of Oil and Gas Substances, as long thereafter as there is production in paying quantities from the leased premises or lands pooled or unitized therewith. After completion of a well capable of producing in paying quantities hereunder, Lessee shall drill such additional wells on the leased premises or lands pooled or unitized therewith as a reasonably prudent operator would drill under the same or similar circumstances to (a) develop the leased premises as to reservoirs then capable of producing in paying quantities on the leased premises or lands pooled or unitized therewith, or (b) protect the leased premises from uncompensated drainage by any well or wells located on other lands not pooled or unitized therewith. There shall be no covenant to drill exploratory wells or any additional wells except as expressly provided herein. As used herein, the term Operations shall mean any activity conducted on or off the leased premises that is reasonably calculated to obtain or restore production, including without limitation, (i) drilling or any act preparatory to drilling (such as obtaining permits, surveying a drill site, staking a drill site, building roads, clearing a drill site, or hauling equipment or supplies); (ii) reworking, plugging back, deepening, treating, stimulating, refitting, installing any artificial lift or production-enhancement equipment or technique; (iii) constructing facilities related to the production, treatment, transportation and marketing of substances produced from the lease premises; (iv) contracting for marketing services and sale of Oil and Gas Substances; and (v) construction of water disposal facilities and the physical movement of water produced from the leased premises.

## Rental Clause

The rental clause of an oil and gas lease describes certain conditions that may be necessary to hold a lease in force during the primary term. If a lease is "paid-up" at the time it is signed, that means that no further payments are required by the Lessee to keep the lease in effect during the primary term. If a lease is not a "paid-up" lease, the Lessee is usually required to make annual delay-rental payments to the Lessor during the primary term if a well is not drilled. If so, the exact amount and place of payment are provided in the rental clause. The amount is often a fixed dollar amount and the place of payment is often a bank.

Some leases specify that if the Lessee makes a good faith error in paying the delay rental, such as the wrong dollar amount or to the wrong location, the Lessor must notify the Lessee and the Lessee has 30 days to correct the payment. This clause has been upheld in Texas, Kincaid v. Gulf Oil Corporation, (Texas Ct. App. 1984).

# Example Rental Clause

If on or before the first anniversary date hereof operations for the drilling of a well for oil or gas or other substances covered hereby have not been commenced on the leased premises or lands pooled or unitized therewith, or if there is no production in paying quantities from the leased premises or lands pooled or unitized therewith, then subject to Paragraph _ this lease shall terminate as to both parties unless Lessee on or before that date pays or tenders to Lessor or to Lessor's credit at ______________, or its successors, which shall be Lessor's depository agent for receiving payments regardless of changes in the ownership of said land, the sum of $____________ as rental covering the privilege of deferring the commencement of operations for the drilling of a well for a period of twelve months from said anniversary date. In like manner and upon like payments or tenders, the commencement of operations for the drilling of a well may be further deferred for one or more twelve-month periods during the primary term of this lease. All payments or tenders may be made in currency, or by check or by draft, and such payments or tenders to Lessor or to the depository by deposit in the U.S. Mail on or before the rental due date in a stamped envelope addressed to the depository or to the Lessor at the last address known to Lessee shall constitute proper payment. If the depository should liquidate or be succeeded by another institution, or for any reason fail or refuse to accept rental payment hereunder, Lessee shall not be held in default for failure to make such payment until 60 days after Lessor has delivered to Lessee a proper recordable instrument naming another institution as depository agent to receive payments. If on or before any rental due date Lessee in good faith makes an erroneous rental payment by paying the wrong person or the wrong depository or the wrong amount, Lessee shall be unconditionally obligated to pay or tender proper rental for the period involved and this lease shall continue in effect as though such rental payment had been properly made, provided that proper rental shall be paid or tendered within 30 days after receipt by Lessee of written notice of the error from Lessor, accompanied by any documents and other evidence necessary to enable Lessee to make proper payment. Lessee may pay or tender any rental at any time in advance of its due date to the Lessor then known to Lessee as provided in Paragraph ____ and such payment or tender shall bind all persons then or thereafter claiming any part of such rental.

## Royalty Clause

The royalty clause of an oil and gas lease describes how the Mineral Interest owner's royalty will be calculated.

Royalties are generally a fixed percentage of the net proceeds of product sales. But adjustments are often made for a Lessor's proportionate share of state and county taxes on the production. Modern royalty clauses often specify that the Lessor's royalty will be calculated from the actual revenue received from the sale of the product rather than the older term which based the royalty calculation on the "market value at the well" which was ambiguous. Generally royalties are free of the cost of bringing oil and gas from the reservoir to the surface. However, Lessors' royalties are often adjusted for their proportionate share of the cost, if any, of moving the product from the well site to the buyer and of any post-production activities such as treating, processing, or compression that is necessary to make the product marketable – regardless of whether those costs are incurred on or off of the lease premises. These clarifications in the royalty clause resulted from Texas

Oil & Gas Corp. v. Vela, (Texas 1968) where an operator was selling gas under a long-term contract at a price that was less than the spot price other operators in the area were receiving for their gas, and from Wood v. TXO Production Corp., (Oklahoma 1992) where the cost of compression as a marketing process came under close scrutiny.

## Example Royalty Clause

For all Oil and Gas Substances that are physically produced from the leased premises, or lands pooled, unitized or communitized therewith, and sold, Lessor shall receive as its royalty 15.00 % of the sales proceeds actually received by lessee or, if applicable, its affiliate, as a result of the first sale of the affected production to an unaffiliated party, less this same percentage share of all Post Production Costs and this same percentage share of all production, severance and ad valorem taxes. As used in this provision, Post Production Costs shall mean all costs actually incurred by lessee or its affiliate and all losses of produced volumes whether by use as fuel, line loss, flaring, venting or otherwise from and after the wellhead to the point of sale. These costs include without limitation, all costs of gathering, marketing, compression, dehydration, transportation, removal of liquid or gaseous substances or impurities from the affected production, and any other treatment or processing required by the first unaffiliated party who purchases the affected production. For royalty calculation purposes, lessee shall never be required to adjust the sales proceeds to account for the purchaser's costs or charges downstream of the point of sale.

Lessee or its affiliate shall have the right to construct, maintain and operate any facilities providing some or all of the services identified as Post Production Costs. If this occurs, the actual costs of such facilities shall be included in the Post Production Costs as a per barrel or per mcf charge, as appropriate, calculated by spreading the construction, maintenance and operating costs for such facilities over the reasonably estimated total production volumes attributable to the well or wells using such facilities.

If Lessee uses the Oil and Gas Substances (other than as fuel in connection with the production and sale thereof) in lieu of receiving sale proceeds, the price to be used under this provision shall be based upon arm's-length sale(s) to unaffiliated parties for the applicable month that are obtainable, comparable in terms of quality and quantity, and in closest proximity to the leased premises. Such comparable arm's-length sales price shall be less any Post Production Costs applicable to the specific arms-length transaction that is utilized.

# Shut-in Royalty Clause

A shut-in royalty clause of an oil and gas lease describes how payments may be made to a Lessor by a Lessee if a well is shut-in. Payment of shut-in royalties allows the Lessee to maintain the lease in full force as if the well were producing in paying quantities. A limiting clause may be included that limits the amount of time that a lease may be maintained by shut-in royalties.

# Example Shut-In Royalty Clause

If after the primary term one or more wells on the leased premises or lands pooled or unitized therewith are capable of producing Oil and Gas Substances in paying quantities, but such well or wells are either shut in or production therefrom is not being sold by Lessee, such well or wells shall nevertheless be deemed to be producing in paying quantities for the purpose of maintaining this lease. If for a period of 90 consecutive days such well or wells are shut in or production therefrom is not sold by Lessee, then Lessee shall pay an aggregate shut-in royalty of one dollar per acre then covered by this lease. The payment shall be made to Lessor on or before the first anniversary date of the lease following the end of the 90-day period and thereafter on or before each anniversary while the well or wells are shut in or production therefrom is not being sold by Lessee; provided that if this lease is otherwise being maintained by operations under this lease, or if production is being sold by Lessee from another well or wells on the leased premises or lands pooled or unitized therewith, no shut-in royalty shall be due until the first anniversary date of the lease following the end of the 90-day period after the end of the period next following the cessation of such operations or production, as the case may be. Lessee's failure to properly pay shut-in royalty shall render Lessee liable for the amount due, but shall not operate to terminate this lease.

## Pooling Clause

A pooling clause in an oil and gas lease enables a Lessee to combine several leases in to a single one-well unit as may be required to meet the spacing requirements of the state oil and gas regulatory agency.

## Example Pooling Clause

Lessee shall have the right but not the obligation to pool all or any part of the leased premises or interest therein with any other lands or interests, as to any or all depths or zones, and as to any or all substances covered by this lease, either before or after the commencement of drilling or production, whenever Lessee deems it necessary or proper to do so in order to prudently develop or operate the leased premises, whether or not similar pooling authority exists with respect to such other lands or interests. The creation of a unit by such pooling shall be based on the following criteria (hereinafter called "pooling criteria"): A unit for an oil well (other than a horizontal completion) shall not exceed 40 acres plus a maximum acreage tolerance of 10%, and for a gas well or a horizontal completion shall not exceed 640 acres plus a maximum acreage tolerance of 10%; provided that a larger unit may be formed for an oil well or gas well or horizontal completion to conform to any well spacing or density pattern that may be prescribed or permitted by any governmental authority having jurisdiction to do so. For the purpose of the foregoing, the terms "oil well" and "gas well" shall have the meanings prescribed by applicable law or the appropriate governmental authority, or, if no definition is so prescribed, "oil well" means a well with an initial gas-oil ratio of less than 100,000 cubic feet per barrel and "gas well" means a well with an initial gas-oil ratio of 100,000 cubic feet or more per barrel, based on a 24-hour production test conducted under normal producing conditions using standard lease separator facilities or equivalent testing equipment; and the term "horizontal completion" means a well in which the horizontal component of the completion interval in the reservoir exceeds the vertical component in such interval. In exercising its pooling rights hereunder, Lessee shall file of record a written declaration describing the unit and stating the effective date of pooling. Production, drilling or reworking operations anywhere on a unit which includes all or any part of the leased premises shall be treated as if it were production, drilling or reworking operations on the leased premises, except that the production on which Lessor's royalty is calculated shall be that proportion of the total unit production which the net acreage covered by this lease and included in the unit bears to the total acreage in the unit, but only to the extent such proportion of unit production is sold by Lessee. In the event a unit is formed hereunder before the unit well is drilled and completed, so that the applicable pooling criteria are not yet known, the unit shall be based on the pooling criteria Lessee expects in good faith to apply upon completion of the well; provided that within a reasonable time after completion of the well, the unit shall be revised if necessary to conform to the pooling criteria that actually exist. Pooling in one or more instances shall not exhaust Lessee's pooling rights hereunder, and Lessee shall have the recurring right but not the obligation to revise any unit formed hereunder by expansion or contraction or both, either before or after commencement of production, in order to conform to the well spacing or density pattern prescribed or permitted by the governmental authority having jurisdiction, or to conform to any productive acreage determination made by such governmental authority. To revise a unit hereunder, Lessee shall file of record a written declaration describing the revised unit and stating the effective date of revision. To the extent any portion of the leased premises is included in or excluded from the unit by virtue of such revision, the proportion of unit production on which royalties are payable hereunder shall thereafter be adjusted accordingly.

## Proportionate Reduction Clause

The proportionate reduction clause of an oil and gas lease allows a Lessee to proportionately reduce royalties and rentals to a Lessor, if the Lessor owns less than 100 percent of the mineral rights in the tract of land where a well is located. It may also stipulate that if any royalty or other payment attributable to the mineral estate is payable to someone other than the Lessor, then it will be deducted from the corresponding amount that would otherwise be payable to the Lessor.

## Example Proportionate Reduction Clause

If Lessor owns less than the full mineral estate in all or any part of the leased premises, payment of royalties and shut-in royalties hereunder shall be reduced as follows: royalties and shut-in royalties for any well on any part of the leased premises or lands pooled therewith shall be reduced to the proportion that Lessor's interest in such part of the leased premises bears to the full mineral estate in such part of the leased premises. To the extent any royalty or other payment attributable to the mineral estate covered by this lease is payable to someone other than Lessor, such royalty or other payment shall be deducted from the corresponding amount otherwise payable to Lessor hereunder.

## Surrender Clause

The surrender clause describes how a Lessee may surrender or release all or part of their interests in a lease to the Lessor.

## Example Surrender Clause

Lessee may, at any time and from time to time, deliver to Lessor or file of record a written release of this lease as to a full or undivided interest in all or any portion of the area covered by this lease or any depths or zones thereunder, and shall thereupon be relieved of all obligations thereafter arising with respect to the interest so released. If Lessee releases less than all of the interest or area covered hereby, Lessee's obligation to pay or tender shut-in royalties shall be proportionately reduced in accordance with the net acreage interest retained hereunder.

## Surface Rights Clause

Although the surface interest is servient to the mineral interest, it is always helpful state specifics in writing. The surface rights clause of an oil and gas lease clearly states the Lessee's rights to use the surface. This includes the rights of ingress and egress on the premises, geophysical operations, drilling wells, building roads, constructing surface production facilities, drilling water wells, disposal wells, and injection wells, adding electrical connections, and the use of water from ponds, lakes, and rivers. Any restrictions on the Lessee's operation are also included such as not operating within 300 feet of a house or a livestock pen. It may also describe a

Lessee's right to pull casing and remove surface production facilities even after a lease has terminated in all other respects.

## Example Surface Rights Clause

The rights granted to Lessee hereunder shall include the right of ingress and egress on the leased premises or lands pooled or unitized therewith, along with such rights as may be reasonably necessary to conduct operations for exploring, developing, producing and marketing Oil and Gas Substances, including but not limited to geophysical operations, the drilling of wells, and the construction and use of roads, canals, pipelines, tanks, water wells, disposal wells, injection wells, pits, electric and telephone lines, power stations, and other facilities deemed necessary by Lessee to explore, discover, produce, store, treat and/or transport Oil and Gas Substances and water produced from the leased premises or other lands that share central facilities and are jointly operated with the leased premises for gathering, treating, compression and water disposal. Lessee may use in such operations, free of cost, any oil, gas, water and/or other substances produced on the leased premises, except water from Lessor's wells or ponds. In exploring, developing, producing or marketing from the leased premises or lands pooled or unitized therewith, the ancillary rights granted herein shall apply (a) to the entire leased premises, notwithstanding any partial release or other partial termination of this lease; and (b) to any other lands in which Lessor now or hereafter has authority to grant such rights in the vicinity of the leased premises or lands pooled or unitized therewith. When requested by Lessor in writing, Lessee shall bury its pipelines below ordinary plow depth on cultivated lands. No well shall be located less than 200 feet from any house or barn now on the leased premises or other lands of Lessor used by Lessee hereunder, without Lessor's consent, and Lessee shall pay for damage caused by its operations to buildings and other improvements now on the leased premises or such other lands, and to commercial timber and growing crops thereon. Lessee shall have the right at any time to remove its fixtures, equipment and materials, including well casing, from the leased premises or such other lands during the term of this lease or within a reasonable time thereafter.

## Unitization Clause

A unitization clause in an oil and gas lease grants the Lessee the right to add the leased premises to a multi-well unit that will include offset leases held by other Operators. This is the first cooperative step that is necessary to initiate a secondary recovery project such as water-flooding where several operators exist in a single field.

# Example Unitization Clause

Lessee shall have the right but not the obligation to commit all or any part of the leased premises or interest therein to one or more unit plans or agreements for the cooperative development or operation of one or more oil and/ or gas reservoirs or portions thereof, if in lessee's judgment such plan or agreement will prevent waste and protect correlative rights, and if such plan or agreement is approved by the federal, state or local governmental authority having jurisdiction. When such a commitment is made, this lease shall be subject to the terms and conditions of the unit plan or agreement, including any formula prescribed therein for the allocation of production from a unit. Upon permanent cessation thereof, Lessee may terminate the unit by filing of record a written declaration describing the unit and stating the date of termination. Pooling hereunder shall not constitute a cross-conveyance of interests.

## Pugh Clause

A Pugh clause in an oil and gas lease limits the acreage in a lease that may be held by production after the primary term.
Any leased lands where wells have not been drilled and operations are not taking place will be released from the lease.

## Example Pugh Clause

If at the end of the primary term, a part but not all of the land covered by this lease, on a surface acreage basis, is not included within a unit or units in accordance with the other provisions hereof, this lease shall terminate as to such part, or parts, of the land lying outside such unit or units, unless this lease is perpetuated as to such land outside such unit or units by operations conducted thereon or by the production of oil, gas or other minerals, or by such operations and such production in accordance with the provisions hereof.

## Depth Clause

A depth clause serves to release depth intervals that are not in use by the Lessor at the end of the primary term.

## Example Depth Clause

At the end of the primary term, or any extension thereof, this lease shall expire and terminate as to all depths lying 200 feet below the base of the deepest producing horizon of any well drilled on the lease premises or on lands pooled therewith during the term of this lease.

# Implied Covenants

In addition to the explicit clauses, there are four implied covenants in oil and gas leases that have been developed from case law. These are unwritten obligations of the Lessee that apply to every oil and gas lease regardless of whether or not they are stated in the lease.

1. An Operator's implied covenant to avoid drainage of a lease to an adjacent lease.

2. An Operator's implied covenant to further development if there is an expectation of profit to the Lessee and the Lessor.

3. An Operator's implied covenant to market produced oil and gas.

4. An Operator's implied covenant to act in good faith.

# Example Oil and Gas Lease

The following is an example of a paid-up oil and gas lease. The original author of this lease is unknown.

## PAID UP OIL AND GAS LEASE

THIS LEASE AGREEMENT is made as of the ___________ day of ___________, 20__ between ______________________ ___________________________________ as Lessor (whether one or more), and __ ________________________________________ ______________, as Lessee. All printed portions of this lease were prepared by the party hereinabove named as Lessee, but all other provisions (including the completion of blank spaces) were prepared jointly by Lessor and Lessee.

1. Grant of Leased Premises. In consideration of a cash bonus in hand paid and the covenants herein contained,

Lessor hereby grants, leases and lets exclusively to Lessee the following described land, hereinafter called leased premises:

(Legal Description Inserted Here)

in the County of ______________________________, State of ______________________________, containing ___________________gross acres, more or less (including any interests therein which Lessor may hereafter acquire by reversion, prescription or otherwise), for the purpose of exploring for, developing, producing and marketing oil and gas, along with all hydrocarbon and non-hydrocarbon substances produced in association therewith ("Oil and Gas Substances"). The term "gas" as used herein includes helium, carbon dioxide, gaseous sulfur compounds, methane produced from coal formations and other commercial gases, as well as normal hydrocarbon gases. In addition to the above-described land, this lease and the term "leased premises" also covers accretions and any small strips or parcels of land now or hereafter owned by Lessor which are contiguous or adjacent to the above-described land, and, in consideration of the aforementioned cash bonus, Lessor agrees to execute at Lessee's request any additional or supplemental instruments for a more complete or accurate description of the land so covered. For the purpose of determining the amount of any payments based on acreage hereunder, the number of gross acres above specified shall be deemed correct, whether actually more or less.

2. Ancillary Rights. The rights granted to Lessee hereunder shall include the right of ingress and egress on the leased premises or lands pooled or unitized therewith, along with such rights as may be reasonably necessary to conduct operations for exploring, developing,

producing and marketing Oil and Gas Substances, including but not limited to geophysical operations, the drilling of wells, and the construction and use of roads, canals, pipelines, tanks, water wells, disposal wells, injection wells, pits, electric and telephone lines, power stations, and other facilities deemed necessary by Lessee to explore, discover, produce, store, treat and/or transport Oil and Gas Substances and water produced from the leased premises or other lands that share central facilities and are jointly operated with the leased premises for gathering, treating, compression and water disposal. Lessee may use in such operations, free of cost, any oil, gas, water and/or other substances produced on the leased premises, except water from Lessor's wells or ponds. In exploring, developing, producing or marketing from the leased premises or lands pooled or unitized therewith, the ancillary rights granted herein shall apply (a) to the entire leased premises, notwithstanding any partial release or other partial termination of this lease; and (b) to any other lands in which Lessor now or hereafter has authority to grant such rights in the vicinity of the leased premises or lands pooled or unitized therewith. When requested by Lessor in writing, Lessee shall bury its pipelines below ordinary plow depth on cultivated lands. No well shall be located less than 200 feet from any house or barn now on the leased premises or other lands of Lessor used by Lessee hereunder, without Lessor's consent, and Lessee shall pay for damage caused by its operations to buildings and other improvements now on the leased premises or such other lands, and to commercial timber and growing crops thereon. Lessee shall have the right at any time to remove its fixtures, equipment and materials, including well casing, from the leased premises or such other lands during the term of this lease or within a reasonable time thereafter.

3. Term of Lease. This lease shall be in force for a primary term of _________ years from the date hereof, and for as long thereafter as oil or gas or other substances covered hereby are produced in paying quantities from the leased premises or from lands pooled or unitized therewith or this lease is otherwise maintained in effect pursuant to the provisions hereof.

4. Operations. If Lessee drills a well which is incapable of producing in paying quantities (hereinafter called "dry hole") on the leased premises or lands pooled or unitized therewith, or if all production (whether or not in paying quantities) permanently ceases from any cause, including a revision of unit boundaries pursuant to the provisions of this lease or the action of any governmental authority, then in the event this lease is not otherwise being maintained in force it shall nevertheless remain in force if Lessee

commences further operations for reworking an existing well or for drilling an additional well or for otherwise obtaining or restoring production on the leased premises or lands pooled or unitized therewith within 90 days after completion of operations on such dry hole or within 90 days after such cessation of all production. If after the primary term this lease is not otherwise being maintained in force, but Lessee is then engaged in Operations, as defined below, this lease shall remain in force so long as any one or more of such Operations are prosecuted with no interruption of more than 90 consecutive days, and if any such Operations result in the production of Oil and Gas Substances, as long thereafter as there is production in paying quantities from the leased premises or lands pooled or unitized therewith. After completion of a well capable of producing in paying quantities hereunder, Lessee shall drill such additional wells on the leased premises or lands pooled or unitized therewith as a reasonably prudent operator would drill under the same or similar circumstances to (a) develop the leased premises as to reservoirs then capable of producing in paying quantities on the leased premises or lands pooled or unitized therewith, or (b) protect the leased premises from uncompensated drainage by any well or wells located on other lands not pooled or unitized therewith. There shall be no covenant to drill exploratory wells or any additional wells except as expressly provided herein. As used herein, the term Operations shall mean any activity conducted on or off the leased premises that is reasonably calculated to obtain or restore production, including without limitation, (i) drilling or any act preparatory to drilling (such as obtaining permits, surveying a drill site, staking a drill site, building roads, clearing a drill site, or hauling equipment or supplies); (ii) reworking, plugging back, deepening, treating, stimulating, refitting, installing any artificial lift or production-enhancement equipment or technique; (iii) constructing facilities related to the production, treatment, transportation and marketing of substances produced from the lease premises; (iv) contracting for marketing services and sale of Oil and Gas Substances; and (v) construction of water disposal facilities and the physical movement of water produced from the leased premises.

5. Shut-in Royalty. If after the primary term one or more wells on the leased premises or lands pooled or unitized therewith are capable of producing Oil and Gas Substances in paying quantities, but such well or wells are either shut in or production therefrom is not being sold by Lessee, such well or wells shall nevertheless be deemed to be producing in paying quantities for the purpose of maintaining this lease. If for a period of 90 consecutive days such well or wells

are shut in or production therefrom is not sold by Lessee, then Lessee shall pay an aggregate shut-in royalty of one dollar per acre then covered by this lease. The payment shall be made to Lessor on or before the first anniversary date of the lease following the end of the 90-day period and thereafter on or before each anniversary while the well or wells are shut in or production therefrom is not being sold by Lessee; provided that if this lease is otherwise being maintained by operations under this lease, or if production is being sold by Lessee from another well or wells on the leased premises or lands pooled or unitized therewith, no shut-in royalty shall be due until the first anniversary date of the lease following the end of the 90-day period after the end of the period next following the cessation of such operations or production, as the case may be. Lessee's failure to properly pay shut-in royalty shall render Lessee liable for the amount due, but shall not operate to terminate this lease.

6. Royalty Payment. For all Oil and Gas Substances that are physically produced from the leased premises, or lands pooled, unitized or communitized therewith, and sold, Lessor shall receive as its royalty _______ % of the sales proceeds actually received by lessee or, if applicable, its affiliate, as a result of the first sale of the affected production to an unaffiliated party, less this same percentage share of all Post Production Costs and this same percentage share of all production, severance and ad valorem taxes. As used in this provision, Post Production Costs shall mean all costs actually incurred by lessee or its affiliate and all losses of produced volumes whether by use as fuel, line loss, flaring, venting or otherwise from and after the wellhead to the point of sale. These costs include without limitation, all costs of gathering, marketing, compression, dehydration, transportation, removal

of liquid or gaseous substances or impurities from the affected production, and any other treatment or processing required by the first unaffiliated party who purchases the affected production. For royalty calculation purposes, lessee shall never be required to adjust the sales proceeds to account for the purchaser's costs or charges downstream of the point of sale.

Lessee or its affiliate shall have the right to construct, maintain and operate any facilities providing some or all of the services identified as Post Production Costs. If this occurs, the actual costs of such facilities shall be included in the Post Production Costs as a per barrel or per mcf charge, as appropriate, calculated by spreading the construction, maintenance and operating costs for such facilities over the reasonably estimated total production volumes attributable to the well or wells using such facilities.

If Lessee uses the Oil and Gas Substances (other than as fuel in connection with the production and sale thereof) in lieu of receiving sale proceeds, the price to be used under this provision shall be based upon arm's-length sale(s) to unaffiliated parties for the applicable month that are obtainable, comparable in terms of quality and quantity, and in closest proximity to the leased premises. Such comparable arm's-length sales price shall be less any Post Production Costs applicable to the specific arms-length transaction that is utilized.

7. Pooling. Lessee shall have the right but not the obligation to pool all or any part of the leased premises or interest therein with any other lands or interests, as to any or all depths or zones, and as to any or all substances covered by this lease, either before or after the commencement of drilling or production, whenever Lessee deems it necessary or

proper to do so in order to prudently develop or operate the leased premises, whether or not similar pooling authority exists with respect to such other lands or interests. The creation of a unit by such pooling shall be based on the following criteria (hereinafter called "pooling criteria"): A unit for an oil well (other than a horizontal completion) shall not exceed 40 acres plus a maximum acreage tolerance of 10%, and for a gas well or a horizontal completion shall not exceed 640 acres plus a maximum acreage tolerance of 10%; provided that a larger unit may be formed for an oil well or gas well or horizontal completion to conform to any well spacing or density pattern that may be prescribed or permitted by any governmental authority having jurisdiction to do so. For the purpose of the foregoing, the terms "oil well" and "gas well" shall have the meanings prescribed by applicable law or the appropriate governmental authority, or, if no definition is so prescribed, "oil well" means a well with an initial gas-oil ratio of less than 100,000 cubic feet per barrel and "gas well" means a well with an initial gas-oil ratio of 100,000 cubic feet or more per barrel, based on a 24-hour production test conducted under normal producing conditions using standard lease separator facilities or equivalent testing equipment; and the term "horizontal completion" means a well in which the horizontal component of the completion interval in the reservoir exceeds the vertical component in such interval. In exercising its pooling rights hereunder, Lessee shall file of record a written declaration describing the unit and stating the effective date of pooling. Production, drilling or reworking operations anywhere on a unit which includes all or any part of the leased premises shall be treated as if it were production, drilling or reworking operations on the leased premises, except that the production on which Lessor's royalty is calculated shall be that proportion of the total unit production which the net acreage covered by this lease and included in the unit bears to the total acreage in the unit, but only to the extent such proportion of unit production is sold by Lessee. In the event a unit is formed hereunder before the unit well is drilled and completed, so that the applicable pooling criteria are not yet known, the unit shall be based on the pooling criteria Lessee expects in good faith to apply upon completion of the well; provided that within a reasonable time after completion of the well, the unit shall be revised if necessary to conform to the pooling criteria that actually exist. Pooling in one or more instances shall not exhaust Lessee's pooling rights hereunder, and Lessee shall have the recurring right but not the obligation to revise any unit formed hereunder by expansion or contraction or both, either before or after commencement of production, in order to conform to the well spacing or density pattern prescribed or permitted by the governmental authority having jurisdiction, or to conform to any productive acreage determination made by such governmental authority. To revise a unit hereunder, Lessee shall file of record a written declaration describing the revised unit and stating the effective date of revision. To the extent any portion of the leased premises is included in or excluded from the unit by virtue of such revision, the proportion of unit production on which royalties are payable hereunder shall thereafter be adjusted accordingly.

8. Unitization. Lessee shall have the right but not the obligation to commit all or any part of the leased premises or interest therein to one or more unit plans or agreements for the cooperative development or operation of one or more oil and/or gas reservoirs or portions thereof, if in lessee's judgment such plan or agreement will prevent waste

and protect correlative rights, and if such plan or agreement is approved by the federal, state or local governmental authority having jurisdiction. When such a commitment is made, this lease shall be subject to the terms and conditions of the unit plan or agreement, including any formula prescribed therein for the allocation of production from a unit. Upon permanent cessation thereof, Lessee may terminate the unit by filing of record a written declaration describing the unit and stating the date of termination. Pooling hereunder shall not constitute a cross-conveyance of interests.

9. Payment Reductions. If Lessor owns less than the full mineral estate in all or any part of the leased premises, payment of royalties and shut-in royalties hereunder shall be reduced as follows: royalties and shut-in royalties for any well on any part of the leased premises or lands pooled therewith shall be reduced

to the proportion that Lessor's interest in such part of the leased premises bears to the full mineral estate in such part of the leased premises. To the extent any royalty or other payment attributable to the mineral estate covered by this lease is payable to someone other than Lessor, such royalty or other payment shall be deducted from the corresponding amount otherwise payable to Lessor hereunder.

10. Ownership Changes. The interest of either Lessor or Lessee hereunder may be assigned, devised or otherwise transferred in whole or in part, by area and/or by depth or zone, and the rights and obligations of the parties hereunder shall extend to their respective heirs, devisees, executors, administrators, successors and assigns. No change in Lessor's ownership shall have the effect of reducing the rights or enlarging the obligations of Lessee hereunder, and no change in ownership shall be binding

on Lessee until 60 days after Lessee has been furnished the original or duly authenticated copies of the documents establishing such change of ownership to the satisfaction of Lessee or until Lessor has satisfied the notification requirements contained in Lessee's usual form of division order. In the event of the death of any person entitled to shut-in royalties hereunder, Lessee may pay or tender such shut-in royalties to the credit of decedent or decedent's estate. If at any time two or more persons are entitled to shut-in royalties hereunder, Lessee may pay or tender such shut-in royalties to such persons either jointly or separately in proportion to the interest which each owns. If Lessee transfers its interest hereunder in whole or in part Lessee shall be relieved of all obligations thereafter arising with respect to the transferred interest, and failure of the transferee to satisfy such obligations with respect to the transferred interest shall not affect the rights of Lessee with respect to any interest not so transferred. If Lessee transfers a full or undivided interest in all or any portion of the area covered by this lease, the obligation to pay or tender shut-in royalties hereunder shall be divided between Lessee and the transferee in proportion to the net acreage interest in this lease then held by each.

11. Release of Lease. Lessee may, at any time and from time to time, deliver to Lessor or file of record a written release of this lease as to a full or undivided interest in all or any portion of the area covered by this lease or any depths or zones thereunder, and shall thereupon be relieved of all obligations thereafter arising with respect to the interest so released. If Lessee releases less than all of the interest or area covered hereby, Lessee's obligation to pay or tender shut-in royalties shall be proportionately reduced in accordance with the net acreage interest retained hereunder.

12. Regulation and Delay. Lessee's obligations under this lease, whether express or implied, shall be subject to all applicable laws, rules, regulations and orders of any governmental authority having jurisdiction, including restrictions on the drilling and production of wells, and regulation of the price or transportation of oil, gas and other substances covered hereby. When drilling, reworking, production or other operations are prevented or delayed by such laws, rules, regulations or orders, or by inability to obtain necessary permits, equipment, services, material, water, electricity, fuel, access or easements, or by fire, flood, adverse weather conditions, war, sabotage, rebellion, insurrection, riot, strike or labor disputes, or by inability to obtain a satisfactory market for production or failure of purchasers or carriers to take or transport such production, or by any other cause not reasonably within Lessee's control, this lease shall not terminate because of

such prevention or delay, and, at Lessee's option, the period of such prevention or delay shall be added to the term hereof. Lessee shall not be liable for breach of any provisions or implied covenants of this lease when drilling, production or other operations are so prevented or delayed.

13. Breach or Default. No litigation shall be initiated by Lessor for damages, forfeiture or cancellation with respect to any breach or default by Lessee hereunder, for a period of at least 90 days after Lessor has given Lessee written notice fully describing the breach or default, and then only if Lessee fails to remedy the breach or default within such period. In the event the matter is litigated and there is a final judicial determination that a breach or default has occurred, this lease shall not be forfeited or cancelled in whole or in part unless Lessee is given a reasonable time after said judicial determination to remedy the breach or

default and Lessee fails to do so.

14. Warranty of Title. Lessor hereby warrants and agrees to defend title conveyed to Lessee hereunder, and agrees that Lessee at Lessee's option may pay and discharge any taxes, mortgages or liens existing, levied or assessed on or against the leased premises. If Lessee exercises such option, Lessee shall be subrogated to the rights of the party to whom payment is made, and, in addition to its other rights, may reimburse itself out of any royalties or shut-in royalties otherwise payable to Lessor hereunder. In the event Lessee is made aware of any claim inconsistent with Lessor's title, Lessee may suspend the payment of royalties and shut-in royalties hereunder, without interest, until Lessee has been furnished satisfactory evidence that such claim has been resolved.

15. Indemnity. Lessee will indemnify and hold Lessor, its officers, directors,

employees, agents, successors and assigns (hereafter collectively referred to as "Indemnified Parties") harmless from any and all claims, demands, suits, losses, damages, and costs (including, without limitation, any attorney fees) incurred by the Indemnified Parties which may be asserted against the Indemnified Parties by reason of or which may arise out of or which may be related to Lessee's activities on the leased premises (including, without limitation, any claims by any owners or lessees of minerals that Lessee's operations hereunder are either illegal, unauthorized, or constitute an improper interference with their rights).

16. Other Provisions. Additional terms of this Lease are set forth on Exhibit A attached hereto and incorporated herein by reference.

# Chapter 12 Oil and Gas Deals

Successfully producing oil and gas from thousands of feet underground and reaping millions of dollars in excess cash requires the cooperation of several people. They include the people who own mineral interests in a tract of land, investors who provide significant amounts of capital, an investment leader, and technical experts such as Geologists, Land Men, Engineers, and Attorneys. Cooperation of these parties toward a common goal suggests that the fruits of success should be distributed equitably between the parties who made it possible. The structuring of oil and gas deals is no more complicated than assigning roles for each of the parties involved and specifying what proportions of the revenue and costs shall be borne by each party and when. There are a myriad of ways to structure oil and gas deals. But over time, certain structures and terms have evolved that are in widespread use. Parties to an oil and gas deal generally fall in to three necessary groups.

**Group 1 – Mineral Interest Owners**

The first group are mineral interest owners. They must first convey their mineral interest in a tract of land to an Operator by executing an oil and gas lease. A single tract of land may have one or many mineral interest owners. Their responsibilities end with the act of executing an oil and gas lease. And their share of any future revenue from a deal is clearly defined by the royalty percentage stated in the royalty clause of the oil and gas lease. Deductions from those royalties for post-production costs and taxes are specified in some leases.

**Group 2 – Working Interest Owners**
The second group of parties to an oil and gas deal are the capital investors. They initially own 100% of the working interest and they provide the cash that is required in a drilling venture. Their initial net revenue interest is 100% minus the mineral interest's royalty in the oil and gas lease. If the mineral interest royalty is 15% then their initial net revenue interest (NRI) is 85%. Capital investors rightly receive the bulk of all revenue generated by a venture.

**Group 3 – The Necessary People**
The third group of parties to an oil and gas deal is everyone else that is necessary to create and begin the effort. These parties may include Geologists,

Geophysicists, Land Men, Engineers, Attorneys, Deal Finders, Deal Creators, and others who provide a professional service. Members of Group 3 initially own 0% of the working interest. However their contributions are necessary and thus the working interest owners set terms in oil and gas deals that provide incentives for these individuals to contribute their time and professional skills to a venture. These incentives include cash, overriding royalty interests, and opportunities to earn a working interest in a well at a later time, at a reduced cost, if certain conditions are met. The opportunity to earn or receive a working interest in a well at a later time, at a reduced cost, if certain conditions are met is called a carried interest.

If you understand the three groups of parties described above and you understand the terminology of: working interest, carried interest, net revenue interest, royalty, and overriding royalty then you will understand 99% of all oil and gas deals. I will now explain these terms to you by first simply defining each of them and then by walking you through the creation of a typical oil and gas deal that employs these terms so you can see how they are used in a real deal. First, here are the definitions.

**Working Interest** - The Lessee's interest in a petroleum property that is created when an oil and gas lease is executed. The working interest is entitled to all revenues from production after subtracting the mineral interest owner's royalty and any overriding royalty interests that the working interest owner has assigned.

**Carried Interest** - Also called a "carry". A carried interest is an interest that is converted to a working interest if and when certain previously negotiated conditions are met. When the conversion occurs, the existing working interest owners jointly and proportionately surrender a portion of their working interest to create room for the new working interest that is owned by the new party. The owner of a carried interest does not receive revenue from that interest and is not liable for costs associated with the interest until the time that the carried interest is converted to a working interest. The three most common conditions or times when a carried interest is converted to a working interest are (1) when a well has been drilled to the casing point, (2) when a well has been drilled and casing and surface facilities have been set and the well is about to begin production ("A Carried Interest Through the Tanks"), and (3) at the time the costs of drilling and completing a well have been recouped by the initial working interest owners or investors. This point in time is also known as "Pay Out" or "Project Pay Out". This third arrangement is known as a Back In After Pay Out (BIAPO).

After the conversion of a carried interest to a working interest occurs, all parties pay their proportionate share of all expenses going forward. The parties are said to be proceeding "Heads Up" which means no one is being carried and everyone is paying their proportionate share of expenses and receiving their proportionate share of the Net Revenue Interest (NRI).

**Net Revenue Interest (NRI)** - The net revenue interest is the revenue interest held in a petroleum property by the working interest owners after the burdens of mineral interest royalty and overriding royalties are subtracted. For example, if an oil company leases a property with a 15% mineral interest royalty, and a 1% overriding royalty interest for the Land Man, then the Net Revenue Interest is 84%.

**Royalty Interest** – A royalty interest owner owns a share of the proceeds from the sale of oil and gas produced from a petroleum property apart from that of the working interest owners. Royalties include Mineral Interest Owner's Royalty which is paid to the land owner or mineral interest owner and Overriding Royalty which is assigned by working interest owners to professionals such as Geologists, Geophysicists, Land Men, and Attorneys who contribute to the initial creation of an oil and gas project in lieu of or in addition to cash compensation.

**Overriding Royalty Interest** - Also known as an ORRI or simply an override. An overriding royalty interest is a revenue interest in a petroleum property that is created by assignment from a working interest. Like a mineral interest owner's royalty, it entitles the owner to a percentage of the revenue from the property free of the costs of production but net of state taxes. An overriding royalty expires when the underlying oil and gas lease expires. Overriding royalty interests are often assigned by working interest owners to professionals such as Geologists, Geophysicists, Land Men, and Attorneys who contribute to the initial creation of an oil and gas project in lieu of or in addition to cash compensation.

# Example Creation of an Oil and Gas Deal with Common Structure and Terms

The following is a walk-through of the creation of a typical oil and gas deal involving the three groups of parties described before and all of the terms discussed above.

First, a person creates an oil company. This person must be experienced in all areas of oil and gas exploration and development. The oil company will be the lead investor and sponsor of the investment and it will be the Operator of the well as defined by the state regulatory agency. The oil company must either generate a prospect internally or purchase a prospect from another party.

We will assume that an Independent Geologist studied the geology of a particular area and (1) researched all of the wells that have already been drilled in the area, (2) created subsurface maps of several productive formations, and (3) cataloged the production histories and decline curves of the previous wells. From this information, the Geologist was able to locate a promising place to drill a new oil well. The proposed well will be 4,200 feet deep with known productive intervals at approximately 1,000 feet, 2,800 feet, and 4,000 feet. Success in just one of these zones would provide an ROI of 3:1 for an investor. And success in more than one zone would yield extraordinary returns. Given its shallow depth and relatively low cost to drill in combination with the high cumulative production of similar wells in the area, the Geologist decides to market his idea and all of the supporting information as a "Prospect". He calls the owner of the oil company and arranges a meeting.

The Geologist shows the prospect to the oil company owner. The oil company owner offers to purchase the prospect from the Independent Geologist for a cash fee of $35,000 payable when the property is leased plus a 2% overriding royalty interest. The Geologist agrees.

The oil company owner calls the state regulatory agency and determines that the minimum drilling and spacing unit is 40 acres. He then checks a land ownership map of the area provided by the county appraisal district and sees that the proposed drilling site falls within a 160-acre plot of land owned by Mr. and Mrs. Smith. The oil company owner studies the county records and finds that Mr. and Mrs. Smith own both the surface rights and the mineral rights to the tract of land.

The oil company hires an Independent Land Man who agrees to be compensated solely by a 1% overriding royalty interest to be granted by the oil company after a lease is executed. The Land Man has decades of experience. He first researches the ownership of the mineral interest in the property and produces a "run sheet". The run sheet shows all of the previous owners of the property and all of the conveyance instruments recorded in the county courthouse from sovereignty through the present. Sovereignty was the time when the land was owned by the government before it was first granted to an individual. The Land Man confirms that Mr. and Mrs. Smith own 100% of the mineral interest in the property. He calls an attorney whom he works with frequently. The attorney writes a title opinion letter stating his opinion that indeed the Smith's have clear title to the mineral interests in the property. The attorney agrees to be paid $1,500 for writing the title opinion letter. The Land Man offers Mr. and Mrs. Smith an oil and gas lease proposal with a 15% royalty. The Smith's counter offer with a 20% royalty. After some back and forth, the two sides agree to an 18% royalty. The oil company leases the entire 160-acre tract of land for three years with a paid up lease. The oil company further agrees to pay a $5,000 lease bonus to the Smith's at the time the lease is signed. The oil and gas lease is executed and filed at the county courthouse. The mineral interest owners, Mr. and Mrs. Smith now have an 18% royalty interest in the lease and the oil company has an 82% net revenue interest (NRI). This means the oil company is entitled to 82% of the revenue from the sales of oil and gas from the lease. But the oil company still has responsibility for 100% of the costs of drilling and producing oil and gas on the lease. So the oil company has a 100% working interest and an 82% net revenue interest (NRI).

However, the oil company owes the Geologist, the Land Man, and the attorney for their contributions in reaching this stage of the investment so it must now meet its obligations.

The oil company pays the Independent Geologist $35,000 and files a document in the county courthouse that grants a 2% overriding royalty interest to the Geologist. This means that the Geologist is entitled to 2% of the gross revenue from the sale of oil and gas from that lease. This 2% overriding royalty interest remains in effect even if the leasehold interest is sold or transferred to another oil company.

Next, the oil company files a document in the county courthouse granting the Land Man a 1% overriding royalty interest in the oil and gas lease. Just like the Geologist's override, this overriding royalty interest remains in place for as long as the oil and gas lease is in effect.

Then the oil company pays the attorney $1,500 cash for writing the title opinion letter.

Next, the oil company hires a Petroleum Engineer to design a well plan and a drilling program. The Engineer decides what bit size to use, what drilling fluid to use, the size and grade of casing to use, the cementing program, what kind of drilling rig to use, a stimulation program, and numerous other technical points and contingencies. The Engineer will also contact contractors and suppliers to assess their availability to perform the work on the proposed well and the costs of their goods and services.

The Engineer will create a document known as an Authorization For Expenditure (AFE). This document itemizes all or most of the expenses that will be incurred in the drilling and completion of the well. It separates dry hole costs from completed well costs and it also separates tangible drilling costs from intangible drilling costs. Tangible drilling costs and intangible drilling costs will be important in our later discussion of oil and gas taxation. Our Engineer agreed to perform all of this planning work for a 1% overriding royalty interest in the oil and gas lease. So as soon as the work is performed, the oil company files a document in the county courthouse granting the Petroleum Engineer a 1% overriding royalty interest in this oil and gas lease.

The oil company still has responsibility for 100% of all costs of the lease and thus still has a 100% working interest. But after having granted a 2% override to the Geologist, a 1% override to the Land Man, and a 1% override to the Engineer, the oil company's net revenue interest has been reduced by 4% from the original 82% to 78%.

Now the oil company requires significant capital to move forward. Several individuals like yourself have contacted the oil company in the past and mentioned that they would like to be contacted the next time the oil company has an investment opportunity available. The oil company contacts you and two other investors. The oil company shows you all of the information about the prospect and offers you an opportunity to invest. After performing your due diligence you decide to invest.

You and the other two investors each agree to pay one third of the costs of drilling and completing the well in return for one third of the working interest, and one third of the net revenue interest subject to a 20% Back In After Pay Out for the oil company. Continue with the assumption that the land owner's royalty is 18% and there is a 4% override. The net revenue interest is 78%. As one of three equal investors you will receive one third of the 78% net revenue interest which is a 26% revenue interest until the project pays out. Pay Out is the time when you have received an amount in payments from oil and gas sales minus operating expenses that is equal to your initial investment that was required to drill and complete the well.

When Pay Out is reached, the oil company will "Back In" for a 20% working interest in the well. From then onward, your working interest changes from one third of 100% (33.33%) to one third of 80% (26.67%). As a result of the 20% Back In After Pay Out, your cost obligations (working interest) change from 33.33% to 26.67%. The same is true for the other two investors. The oil company's working interest increases from 0% to 20%. The total working interest is always 100%.

Now let's see the affect of the 20% Back In on the net revenue interests. Prior to Pay Out, each of the three investors had a 26% revenue interest. Three times 26% is 78%. 78% was the net revenue interest. The remaining 22% was held by mineral interest royalty and overriding royalties.

The Back In After Pay Out entitles the oil company to 20% of the 78% net revenue interest which is a 15.6% revenue interest. The three investors each then have one third of the remaining 80% of the original 78% which is 62.4%. One third of 62.4% means each investor now has a 20.8% revenue interest for the remaining life of the well.

20.8% Per investor times three investors equals 62.4% plus the 15.6% for the oil company equals the original 78% net revenue interest. The remaining 22% are still held by the mineral interest owner and the override which never change and are unaffected by the back in after pay out.

A "Back In" does not have to occur at all and it does not have to occur at the time of Pay Out. Oil deals may or may not include a carried interest but if they do, they are usually set to occur at one of three times: "The casing point", "Through the tanks", or at "Pay Out".

## Carried Interest To the Casing Point

The first time that a carried interest may be converted to a working interest is at the casing point. This is called a carried interest to the casing point. Under this arrangement a carried interest owned by a party in Group 3 is "carried" free of cost for that party up to the time that a well has been drilled to its total depth and a decision is being made to run casing and attempt to produce the well or to plug and abandon the well as a dry hole. If the decision is made to plug the well, the party with the carried interest does not bear any costs. However, if a decision is made to run casing, then the carried interest is converted to a working interest at that moment. Typical carried interests are 20% to 25% but they can be any amount that the parties agree to in advance. For this example, we will assume that the oil company had a 20% carried interest to the casing point. This means the oil company would have a 20% working interest going forward and would pay 20% of all costs including 20% of the immediate cost of running production casing and cementing it. The oil company would also receive 20% of the total net revenue interest. The other working interest owners would see both their working interests (cost obligations) and net revenue interests (revenue) change to 80% of their prior amount.

## Carried Interest Through the Tanks

The second way that a carried interest is set is "through the tanks". Under this arrangement the oil company's or another party's interest is "carried" up to the time that a well has been drilled to its total depth, casing has been run, surface facilities have been set and production begins. The tanks that are referred to in the phrase "through the tanks" are the stock tanks on the surface that are used to store oil between the time it is brought to the surface and the time it is hauled away in a tanker truck. The party with the carried interest backs in for a working interest at the moment that production begins. Typical carried interests are 20% to 25% but they can be any amount that the parties agree to in advance. For this example, we will assume that the oil company had a 20% carried interest "through the tanks". This means the oil company would have a 20% working interest and would pay 20% of all costs incurred after production begins. The oil company would also receive 20% of the original net revenue interest (20% of the original 78% Net Revenue Interest). The other working interest owners would see both their working interests (cost obligations) and net revenue interests (revenue) change to 80% of their prior amount.

# Back In After Pay Out

The third arrangement is a Back In After Pay Out (BIAPO). This was the arrangement first described above. Under this arrangement the oil company's interest is "carried" up to the time a well pays out for the investors. When this point in time is reached, the party with the carried interest backs in for a working interest. Again, typical carried interests are 20% to 25% but they can be any amount that the parties agree to in advance. For this example, we will assume that the oil company had a 20% carried interest with a "Back In After Pay Out". This means the oil company would acquire a 20% working interest and would pay 20% of all costs incurred after the time that Pay Out occurs. The oil company would also receive 20% of the original net revenue interest (20% of the original 78% Net Revenue Interest). The other working interest owners would see both their working interests (cost obligation) and net revenue interests (revenue) change to 80% of their prior amount.

## Limiting Liability

Liability can be limited for the individual investor if a deal is structured as a Limited Partnership with the Lead Investor's C-Corporation being the General Partner of the Limited Partnership and with that C-Corporation owning a 1% interest in the Limited Partnership. The remaining 99% interest in the Limited Partnership can be divided up as Limited Partnership interests between the Individual Investors and the Operator as they please.

# Joint Operating Agreement (JOA)

All of the terms under which you will operate the well with the oil company are written in a Joint Operating Agreement (JOA) which is signed by you, the oil company, and the each of the other investors. Joint Operating Agreements are widely used across the oil and gas industry. The most common JOA forms are the AAPL Form 610-1982 and AAPL Form 610-1989. These forms are available from all oil and gas attorneys and they can be purchased online for a few hundred dollars.

# Capital

Oil and gas projects are funded in several ways depending on their size.

## Individual Investors

Projects requiring $100,000 to $2 million are funded by individuals. Most readers of this book will be directly investing in projects of this size.

## Oil and Gas Exploration Companies

The next tier in project size is $10 million to $100 million. These projects are funded by oil and gas exploration and production companies. They include both private and public companies. You probably noticed that we did not include project sizes of $2 million to $10 million in either the first or second tier. This is because there is a shortage of capital for projects in this range. They are too big for most individual investors and too small for all of the other sources of capital.

## Banks, Mezzanine Finance Companies, and Private Equity

Banks, mezzanine finance companies, and private equity can provide capital in the third tier which is roughly $10 million to $150 million.

## Public Equity and Public Debt

Finally, public equity and public debt can be accessed for projects of $100 million and up - preferably much more.

# Chapter 13 Economic Evaluation of Oil and Gas Deals

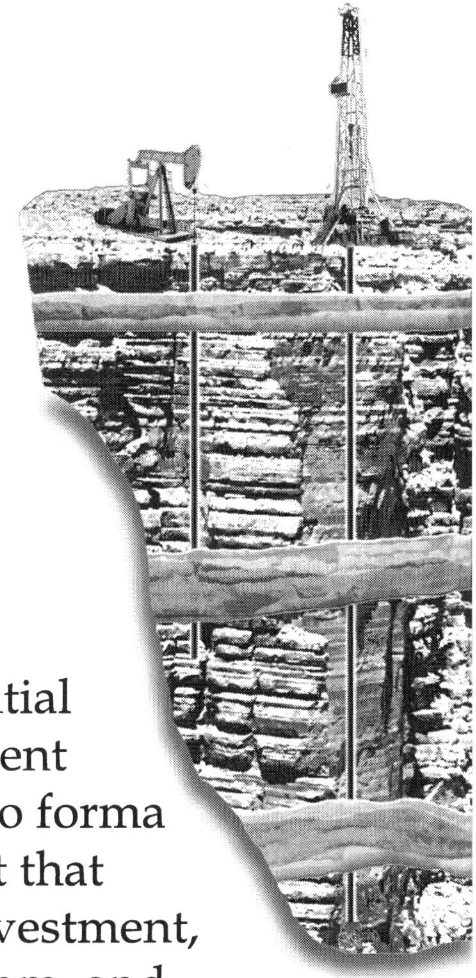

To evaluate a potential oil and gas investment you must have a pro forma cash flow statement that shows the initial investment, future revenue stream, and all operating expenses that will exist throughout the life of a property. Then you apply the three metrics of (1) Return on Investment, (2) Discounted Cash Flow Rate of Return, and (3) Net Present Value to the pro forma cash flow statement. Repeating this process with all of the investment opportunities that you review will illuminate those opportunities that have the best returns.

## Pro Forma Cash Flow Statement

A proforma cash flow is a spread sheet that begins with a listing of projected monthly production volumes of oil and natural gas over the life of a well or a group of wells. The production rate over time will depend on the reservoir drive mechanism. Review the chapter about reservoir drive mechanisms for more information. You must have a justifiable initial production rate and a predicted decline rate for your well or wells. Approximately 80% of all wells have annual production decline rates that are between 12% and 30%. To say it another way, in any given year, 80% of all wells produce between 70% and 88% of the amount that they produced in the prior year.

The remaining 20% of wells have decline rates that are either higher or lower. If analogous offset wells have already been drilled in the formation you are targeting then you can use the decline rates observed in those wells unless you have better information. The decline rates can be found by plotting publicly available production histories.

Next, you must estimate the sales prices of the crude oil and natural gas you will sell over time. This is an opportunity to be either conservative or optimistic. If you have very large production volumes, futures contracts can be used as a price hedge for perhaps half of your expected production.

Multiplying the estimated production volume for each month by the projected sales price per barrel of oil or per mcf of gas for that month will give you a projected gross income for each month during the life of the well. From this gross income you must subtract the mineral interest's royalty and any overriding royalty interests that may be assigned to a Geologist, Engineer, Land Man, Attorney or other person.

Next you must subtract state and local production taxes (severance taxes and or ad valorem taxes). Then you subtract operating costs to yield the net operating income for the well. The costs of workovers from time to time and the costs of ultimately plugging and abandoning the well are part of the operating costs. It is this stream of monthly and annual net operating income that you will use to evaluate the financial strength of the investment.

The numbers used in a pro forma cash flow statement vary from person to person based on their interpretation of the production history of similar wells, the assumed product sales prices, assumed future operating expenses, differences of plans between operators regarding how to drill and produce wells, and the value assigned to possible oil and gas reserves in a reservoir that a well may have penetrated but has not yet produced (reserves behind pipe).

## Return-on-Investment (ROI)

The first metric used to evaluate a potential investment is Return-on-Investment (ROI). Summing the Net Operating Income for the entire life of the well and dividing it by the initial cost of leasing, surveying, drilling, completing, stimulating the well, and placing it on production yields your Return-on-Investment (ROI).

Investors should require a Return-on-Investment of at least 2:1 or 3:1 and but much higher ROI's do happen.

# Discounted-Cash-Flow-Rate-of-Return (DCFROR)

The Discounted Cash Flow Rate of Return (DCFROR), also known as the Internal Rate of Return (IRR), is the annual discount rate that the net operating income must be discounted by to force the ROI to be 1:1. Determining DCFROR is an iterative process but it is very easy.

To determine DCFROR of a cash flow, you must first know the total cost of initiating production for your project. This includes all land, leasehold, legal, geology, seismic, drilling, completion, stimulation, and pipeline costs.

The next step is to arbitrarily choose a discount percentage such as 30% and then divide the first year's net operating income by $(1.30)^1$. Note that the exponent is equal to the year that the net income was received. The exponent is 1 for the first year, 2 for the second year, 3 for the third year, and so on.

Continuing forward, divide the second year's net operating income by $(1.30)^2$. Divide the third year's net operating income by $(1.30)^3$. Divide the fourth year's net operating income by $(1.30)^4$. Continue this for all years that the well(s) will be productive. The exponent in the denominator increases with each year. So the revenue far in the future will be discounted much more than revenue from the first few years. Sum these discounted cash amounts for all years. If the summation of all of the discounted amounts for all years is equal to the total cost of initiating production then you have correctly determined that the Discounted Cash Flow Rate of Return is 30%.

However, if the summation of these discounted amounts for all years is greater than the total cost of initiating production then your estimate of 30% was too low and you must try again with a higher discount number - say 35%. You will repeat the process using 35%.

Divide the first year's net operating income by $(1.35)^1$. Then divide the second year's net operating income by $(1.35)^2$. Divide the third year's net operating income by $(1.35)^3$. Divide the fourth year's net operating income by $(1.35)^4$. Continue this for all years that the well(s) will be productive. Sum these discounted cash amounts for all years. If the summation of these discounted amounts is equal to the total cost of initiating production then you have determined that the Discounted Cash Flow Rate of Return is 35%. Keep changing the discount rate in your spreadsheet until the total cost of initiating production exactly equals the summation of the discounted amounts for all years that the well or wells will be producing.

## Net Present Value

The third metric for evaluating a pro forma cash flow statement is the Net Present Value (NPV). The Net Present Value of a cash flow is the net operating income you will receive over the life of the well minus the initial cost of leasing, surveying, drilling, completing, stimulating the well, and placing it on production with that net amount then being discounted to account for the diminishing value of the dollar over time.

Typically this is done by discounting the net operating income by 10% annually. For example, you would divide the first year's net operating income by $(1.10)^1$. Then you would divide the second year's net operating income by $(1.10)^2$. Then you would divide the third year's net operating income by $(1.10)^3$. And you would divide the fourth year's net operating income by $(1.10)^4$ and so on.

The summation of these net operating incomes for all productive years by this method minus all of the initial costs of creating the well would yield the "Net Present Value at a 10% Discount". This method can be used with any discount number you choose but 10% is a common number in the industry.

## Risk

Be sure to include a risk factor to discount the total return to reflect the odds of success in finding oil and gas. For example, if you will be investing in a series of 10 new wells to be drilled and you believe the odds of success in finding oil and gas in each well is 80%, then your calculations should include eight successful wells and two dry holes.

# Final Analysis

All of these calculations are Before-Federal-Income-Tax. By comparing the Return-On-Investment, the Discounted-Cash-Flow-Rate-of-Return, and the Net Present Value for various opportunities you can decide which ones you will invest in and which ones you will pass on.

# Chapter 14 Oil and Gas Taxation

The two most important parts of oil and gas taxation are (1) the 100% deduction of intangible drilling costs in the first year, and (2) the depletion deduction which reduces the taxes you pay on revenue from production. A depletion deduction can be calculated by one of two methods: Percentage Depletion or Cost Depletion. In this chapter we will first discuss the 100% deduction of intangible drilling costs and then we will discuss both methods of calculating the depletion deduction. Many of the excerpts in this chapter about Intangible Drilling Costs, Percentage Depletion, and Cost Depletion were taken directly from the IRS.

## Deducting Intangible Drilling Costs

The costs of developing oil and gas wells are ordinarily capital expenditures. You can usually recover them through depreciation or depletion. However, you can elect to deduct intangible drilling costs (IDC's) as a current business expense. These are only for drilling and development costs for wells in the United States in which you hold an operating or working interest. You can deduct only costs for drilling or preparing a well for the production of oil or gas. You can elect to deduct only the costs of items with no salvage value. These include wages, fuel, repairs, hauling, and supplies related to drilling wells and preparing them for production. Your cost for any drilling or development work done by contractors under any form of contract is also an intangible drilling cost (IDC). If you do not elect to deduct your IDCs as a current business expense, you can elect to deduct them over the 60-month period beginning with the month they were paid or incurred.

You can elect to deduct IDCs as a current business expense by taking the deduction on your income tax return for the first tax year you have eligible costs. No formal statement is required. If you file Schedule C (Form 1040), enter these costs under "Other expenses." For oil and gas wells, your election is binding for the year it is made and for all later years.

# Depletion Deduction

Depletion provides for the recovery of a capital investment over time. Percentage depletion is a tax deduction that is calculated by applying an allowable percentage to the gross income from a property. For oil and natural gas the allowable percentage is 15 percent. This means that 15% of a petroleum property's revenue from product sales is tax free. The law limits the use of the 15% allowable for percentage depletion of oil and gas in several ways.

# Limits

First, the percentage depletion allowance may only be taken by independent producers and royalty owners and not by integrated oil companies.

Second, depletion may only be claimed up to production levels of 1,000 barrels per day of oil or 6,000 mcf per day of natural gas.

Third, the deduction is limited to 65% of net taxable income.

Fourth, the net income limitation requires percentage depletion to be calculated on a property-by-property basis. It prohibits percentage depletion to the extent that it exceeds the net income from an individual property.

These limitations apply both for regular and alternative minimum tax purposes. Percentage depletion in excess of the 65 percent limit may be carried over to future years until it is fully utilized.

## Depletion Discussion

Depletion is the using up of natural resources through production. The depletion deduction allows an owner or operator to account for the reduction of a property's reserves.

If you have an economic interest in mineral property, you can take a deduction for depletion.

You have an economic interest if both of the following apply.

1. You have acquired by investment any interest in mineral deposits.

2. You have a legal right to income from the extraction of the mineral to which you must look for a return of your capital investment.

Mineral property includes oil and gas wells, mines, and other natural deposits. For this purpose, the term "property" means each separate interest you own in each mineral deposit in each separate tract or parcel of land. You can treat two or more separate interests as one property or as separate properties. See section 614 of the Internal Revenue Code and the related regulations for rules on how to treat separate mineral interests. There are two ways of figuring depletion on a mineral property: (1) Percentage Depletion, and (2) Cost Depletion.

Percentage depletion can only be used by independent producers or royalty owners and most independent producers use percentage depletion.

## Percentage Depletion

To figure percentage depletion, you multiply a certain percentage (currently 15% for oil and gas) by your gross income from the property during the tax year.

When figuring your percentage depletion, you can first subtract from your gross income any rents or royalties you paid or incurred for the property.

Generally, you figure your percentage depletion by computing your average daily production of domestic oil or gas and comparing it to your depletable oil or gas quantity. There will be more on "depletable oil or gas quantity" in a moment. If your average daily production does not exceed your depletable oil or gas quantity (and it probably will not), you figure your percentage depletion by multiplying the gross income from the oil or gas property by 15%.

Your depletable oil quantity is 1,000 barrels. This simply means that there is a limit of 1,000 barrels per day upon which you can apply a 15% percentage depletion. Your default depletable natural gas quantity is zero. If you produce both oil and natural gas, you must reduce the 1,000 barrel oil per day limit to create a depletable natural gas quantity. Your depletable natural gas quantity is 6,000 cubic feet per day multiplied by the number of barrels that you reduce your depletable oil quantity by to make room for natural gas production. If you converted all of your oil allowance to a natural gas allowance you would have a limit of 1000 x 6,000 cubic feet per day for a total of 6,000 mcf per day.

## Example Reduction of Your Depletable Oil Quantity to Create a Depletable Quantity of Natural Gas

You have both oil and natural gas production. To figure your depletable natural gas quantity, you choose to apply 360 barrels per day of your 1000 barrel per day depletable oil quantity toward gas. Your depletable natural gas quantity is (360 × 6000) = 2.16 million cubic feet of gas per day. You must reduce your depletable oil quantity to 640 barrels per day (1000 – 360).

## Partnerships

Generally, each partner or shareholder, and not the partnership, figures the depletion allowance separately. The partnership must allocate to each partner or shareholder his or her share of the adjusted basis of each oil or gas property held by the partnership. Each partner's share of the adjusted basis of the oil or gas property generally is figured according to that partner's interest in the partnership.

Each partner or shareholder must separately keep records of his or her share of the adjusted basis in each oil and gas property of the partnership. The partner must reduce his or her adjusted basis by the depletion allowed or allowable on the property each year. The partner or shareholder must use that reduced adjusted basis to figure cost depletion or his or her gain or loss if the partnership disposes of the property.

Information that you, as a partner, use to figure your depletion deduction on oil and gas properties is reported by the partnership on Schedule K-1 (Form 1065). Deduct oil and gas depletion for your partnership interest on Schedule E (Form 1040). The depletion deducted on Schedule E is included in figuring income or loss from rental real estate or royalty properties.

## Cost Depletion

The second method of calculating a depletion deduction for federal income taxes is cost depletion. This method is seldom used by independent producers because it is far more complex than percentage depletion and it usually provides a smaller deduction than percentage depletion.

To figure cost depletion you must first determine the following.

A. The property's basis for depletion.
B. The total recoverable units of mineral in the property's natural deposit.
C. The number of units of mineral sold during the tax year.

**Step 1. Determining the Property's Basis for Depletion**

To determine the property's basis for depletion, subtract all of the following from the property's adjusted basis.

1. Amounts recoverable through:
    a. Depreciation deductions,
    b. Deferred expenses (including deferred exploration and development costs), and
    c. Deductions other than depletion.
2. The residual value of land and

improvements at the end of operations.

3. The cost or value of land acquired for purposes other than mineral production.

The adjusted basis of your property is your original cost or other basis, plus certain additions and improvements, and minus certain deductions such as depletion allowed or allowable and casualty losses. Your adjusted basis can never be less than zero.

### Step 2. Determining the Total Recoverable Units of Mineral in the Property's Natural Deposit

The total recoverable units is the sum of the following:

- The number of units of mineral remaining at the end of the year (including units recovered but not sold).

- The number of units of mineral sold during the tax year (determined under your method of accounting, as explained next).

You must estimate or determine recoverable units (barrels, thousands of cubic feet) of mineral products using the current industry method and the most accurate and reliable information you can obtain.

**Step 3. Determining the Number of Units of Minerals Sold During the Tax Year**

You determine the number of units sold during the tax year based on your method of accounting.

If you use the cash method of accounting then the units sold during the year are the units sold for which you receive payment during the tax year (regardless of the year of sale).

If you use the accrual method of accounting then the units sold during the year are the units sold based on your inventories and method of accounting for inventory.

The number of units sold during the tax year does not include any for which depletion deductions were allowed or allowable in earlier years.

**Step 4. Calculating the Cost Depletion Deduction**

Once you have performed the first three steps of determining the property's basis for depletion, the total recoverable units, and the number of units sold during the tax year, you can figure your cost depletion deduction by doing the following:

Divide your property's basis for depletion by the total recoverable units and then multiply this term by the units sold during the tax year. The result is your cost depletion deduction.

Congratulations, you've calculated your cost depletion deduction. Again, most independent oil and gas companies and their investors use percentage depletion rather than cost depletion.

# Chapter 15

# Presentation of a Prospect

When an Operator presents a prospect to you as a potential investor, they will often first provide a brief description of the prospect by a telephone call, meeting, or a one-page description by mail or email. This will describe generally where the prospect is located, geologic targets, well depth, reservoir pressure, reservoir size, whether it will produce oil or gas, surface restrictions, the general risk level, the net revenue interest, and the proposed deal terms.

If you are interested in seeing more, the Operator may follow the first brief with a second meeting or telephone call and provide a detailed brochure. The detailed brochure should include cost estimates of leases, seismic, location, drilling, completion, production facilities, and pipelines. It should also describe the surface access and any necessary permits. Additionally it should include gas pipeline locations, a land map, reserve estimates, a geologic description, all available maps, seismic, logs, production histories, and the proposed deal terms.

# Part III

# 150 Questions to Consider Before You Invest

If you are considering an oil and gas investment proposal, then what you need most is help deciding whether or not to invest. The following is a list of questions to consider before you invest. I have categorized the list in to questions about the reservoir, questions about the land, questions about the well, legal questions, and financial questions.

Your purpose in considering these questions is to learn everything about the investment that is knowable, to identify those things that are unknowable, and to determine what if anything is probable.

These are good questions to ponder alone or to ask the investment sponsor.

The answers to these questions will help you more thoroughly understand the investment you are considering and the people who are sponsoring it.

You will then be in the optimum position to decide GO or NO GO.

# Chapter 16 Questions about the Reservoir

Why do you think there is oil or gas in this location and at this depth?

If the well is a dry hole, what will be the most likely explanation?

Likely answers are that the formation will have been too low, too thin, not there, faulted out, or there was no trap. If the formation was there but it was 100% saturated with water it will be described as “wet”.

❓Is this prospect in a well-known producing region or is it a more exploratory prospect? This is a basic question. Refer to the map on the opposite page.

Are you drilling in an area where a lot of other successful oil and gas wells have been drilled or not? If all other factors are equal, you are much more likely to drill a successful oil and gas well if you are drilling in an area where nearby wells have produced oil and natural gas. This is because those wells and the oil and gas they have produced provide strong evidence that source rocks that produce oil and gas - and reservoir rocks that trap and accumulate oil and gas - exist in the area. This is evidence that the geologic prerequisites for success are in place.

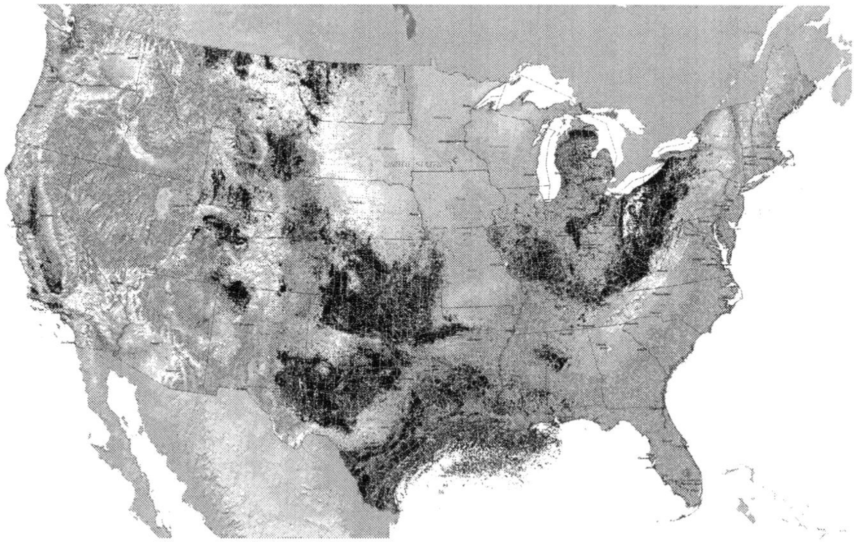

The blackened portions of this map represent areas where oil or natural gas wells have been successfully drilled and produced in the U.S.

Do I have a map that shows all of the other wells, both successful wells and dry holes that have been drilled in the area in my target reservoirs?

The Operator should have such a map. It will be a zoomed-in (larger scale) version of the map above for your prospect area. You can obtain your own map of the prospect area from the state regulatory agency. Refer to the oil and gas web sites section at the back of this book.

What is the projected cumulative production for each potential pay zone in the proposed well?

What were the cumulative productions of nearby wells that produced from the same intervals? This is an important reality check.

What reservoir drive mechanism is expected in this reservoir: depletion drive, gas cap drive, solution gas drive, water drive, gravity drainage?

Are there any dry holes nearby? How far away are they? Did they penetrate the zone of interest? Will we be up-dip to those wells? No matter where you are, there will always be a dry hole somewhere. It may be near or far.

What are the drainage areas of the nearby wells? Is it possible that those wells have already drained the area where we will drill? The more permeable the rock and the fewer variations there are within the rock, the wider the drainage area. The Operator should have a plausible reason for believing that the area has not been drained. For example they may say that all of the wells in this area are drilled on a 40-acre spacing and they have been shown to produce about 30,000 barrels of oil per well. Or they may say that that the new well will be in a different fault block and thus you will be producing from a separate reservoir.

What are the target formations?

What are the lithologies of the target formations? Are they sandstones, conglomerates, limestones, dolomites, chalk, shales, cherts?

Under what depositional environments were these formations deposited?

What are the geologic ages of the target formations and the formations above and below them?

What tectonic events if any have impacted these formations by compression or extension after they were deposited?

What are the expected porosities of the target formations?

Is there any secondary porosity? Secondary porosity is void space within the rock that was created after the original deposition of the sediments such as: fractures, vugs, pore space caused by dissolution of minerals, and bioturbation.

Are the formations brittle or ductile? If brittle, is it important for the rock to be brittle so that fractures are present? Many formations produce at much higher rates when natural fractures are present.

❓What are the permeabilities of the target formations? Admittedly, knowing the permeability is less important than knowing the production rates, decline characteristics, and cumulative productions of analogous wells but it can help you get a feel for the rock you are working in.

❓Are the formations competent or unconsolidated?

❓Are the grains well sorted or poorly sorted?

❓Is there any shale or clay content in the formation?

❓Are the traps expected to be structural traps or stratigraphic traps?

❓What is the strike and dip of the formation in this location?
Is it high-angle or low-angle dip?

❓If the traps are structural, are they anticlines, fault traps, salt dome traps, or unconformity traps?

❓Are these the same kinds of traps that exist in the reservoirs of the nearby wells? Why or why not?

❓Can the subsurface map be drawn in any other way? If so, how? Subsurface maps can always be drawn in another way. This is one of the primary risks you are facing. How many factors are supporting the drawing of the subsurface map in the way it is currently drawn?

❓What are the log characteristics of a successful well and an unsuccessful well? What are the likely readings of the gamma ray, spectral gamma ray, density porosity, neutron porosity, resistivity, acoustic, magnetic resonance, 3D resistivity, borehole imaging logs, and elemental composition logs?

Will you take wireline fluid samples? What are the characteristics of a wireline fluid sample in a successful well?

Will you take any cores in this well? What are the characteristics of a sidewall core, rotary core, or whole core in a successful well?

What is the expected reservoir temperature? What is the temperature gradient? Are there any depths along the projected wellbore path where the temperature gradient changes? Temperature affects the phase behavior (gas or liquid) of a fluid. Temperature affects the viscosity of a fluid down hole. Temperature also affects what types of logging equipment can be used in a well. And temperature affects the rate that cement sets. Be sure to account for temperature and any uncertainty of the temperature in your cementing program. Temperatures can be measured with open hole logs. And monitoring the temperature of mud returns at the surface is one way to detect when you are entering an over-pressured interval. The temperature gradient may change as you drill in to an over-pressured interval.

What is the expected reservoir pressure? Is it normally pressured or over-pressured? Pore pressure determines the mud density that must be used. And the fracture gradient determines the upper limit of the mud weight that can be used. Pressure also affects the downhole and surface equipment that must be used. Equipment for higher pressure costs more.

Is the fluid likely to be oil or gas or both? Is it a live oil, a dead oil, dry gas, a condensate gas, or a retrograde gas?

If oil, will it contain dissolved gas that will bubble out of solution at surface pressure and temperature?

If oil, what is the likely API gravity?

Will the gas that is separated out of the oil be sold or flared?

If the well will produce oil, what is the bubble point pressure of the oil at reservoir temperature?

If the well will produce gas, will it be dry gas or wet gas?

If it is a wet gas (also called a condensate gas), at what pressure and temperature conditions will liquids begin to precipitate out of the gas stream? Will this occur in the wellbore? How will this affect production? Will the gas be able to lift the liquid out of the well or will the liquid accumulate in the wellbore?

If it is a wet gas, how will it be separated at the surface and how will the liquid and gaseous hydrocarbons be sold?

- What is the btu content of the gas? This affects the price that you will receive when you sell your gas.

- Will the Operator obtain a downhole fluid sample from the reservoir using wireline tools during the open hole logging operation? Will the sample be sent to a laboratory for analysis or will it simply be observed and discarded?

- Is there an aquifer or water zone near the hydrocarbon reservoir?

- If there is a nearby water zone, what are the odds that it will interfere with hydrocarbon production?

- If there is a nearby water zone, will special precautions be necessary to avoid the production of water from that zone in to the wellbore?

How much will it cost to workover the well to recomplete it from producing in the first pay zone to producing from the second pay zone? This will be part of your future operating costs.

Does the Operator expect to use secondary or tertiary recovery methods?

If the Operator plans to create a waterflood, is the formation oil wet or water wet?

Is there $H_2S$ in the area? Is it a concern on this well?

Is there $CO_2$ in the gas? $CO_2$ can hasten corrosion of downhole equipment.

# Chapter 17 Questions about the Land

**?** Are we going to drill a new well on a tract of land where there is no existing production or are we purchasing a lease where there is already one or more producing wells?

These are two different kinds of deals. We will discuss both. If you are purchasing existing production then your venture is competing with smart experienced people. Both your team and your competitors will plot the monthly production of the wells versus time from the day the well began producing to the present. If flowing tubing pressures are available, you will plot these as well. Both your team and your competitors will analyze the production history through a method called decline curve analysis to determine the reservoir drive mechanism and estimate the amount of oil or gas that the well will produce between now and the time it reaches its economic limit. Each of you will reach slightly different but relatively close estimates of how much oil or gas remains to be produced. You will also reach slightly different estimates of how much revenue you will receive from the sale of the production and the operating costs you will incur in producing it. From these analyses your team will makes its offer. If you are negotiating with a reasonable seller you may come out well. But if you are bidding against smart, experienced, well-capitalized buyers in an auction environment then it is far more difficult to get a great deal. The only way to have an edge in this kind of situation is to know something others don't. You might know that a certain zone behind pipe can be produced or that the producing zone would respond well to a hydraulic fracture treatment, or that a major oil company will be coming though the area and drilling very deep wells and you will allow them to farm in to the lease.

When purchasing existing production it is important for you to determine the reservoir drive mechanism because some drive mechanisms provide a long predictable decline in production which you can confidently bid on while others subject you to sudden death meaning that your production will suddenly change from a high rate to zero in a matter of days when water reaches the perforations. Water drive is the best drive mechanism for oil but it is the worst drive mechanism for gas. Water drive gas reservoirs are sudden death. Depletion drive (volumetric) is the best drive mechanism for gas reservoirs. The production histories for most wells are publicly available. Ask the state oil and gas regulatory agency.

If you are drilling new wells on a tract of land where no production currently exists then you have a higher risk proposition but you may receive a higher return on your investment if you are successful in finding an oil and gas reservoir.

❓Is there a single oil and gas lease that covers all of the acreage or are there multiple oil and gas leases over multiple tracts of land? The prospect may include only a single tract of land or many tracts of land. All of the tracts of land may be owned by a single mineral interest owner or each tract of land may be owned by a different mineral interest owner. And any one tract of land can be owned by a group of mineral interest owners who each own an undivided interest in the property. An oil and gas lease may include one or more tracts of land and may have one or more signatures from one or more mineral interest owners. You want to be sure that you have oil and gas leases for all of the tracts of land that are involved and you want to be sure you have signatures from all of the mineral interest owners of each tract of land.

❓Do the leases have a pooling clause that will allow for pooling of adjacent tracts of land if necessary? If the oil and gas leases allow for pooling then it will be easier to drill wells near the boundaries of individual tracts of land.

❓Do the tracts of land form a contiguous area? If the leases form a contiguous area then you may be able to set centralized production facilities on the lease if you have multiple wells. If the terms of the oil and gas lease will not allow this then you will have to set multiple surface facilities.

Are there any tracts of land that have multiple oil and gas leases signed by multiple partial owners in the same tract of land? Your ultimate goal here is to be certain that you have good title to all of the land. The Operator should have or obtain a title opinion letter before substantial investments are made. A Land Man or a Title Company are both sources of help. You will want to see a run sheet showing all of the title conveyance documents for the property from sovereignty (the time the land was owned by the state) to the present.

Are the oil and gas leases recorded in the county courthouse? If the land is leased and the lease has been recorded, the Operator should be able to provide you with a copy of the lease and you should be able to independently obtain a copy of the lease from the county courthouse. If the lease is not recorded, why not? Some oil and gas leases are not recorded when the Operator has obtained some but not all of the signatures of a group of people who have undivided mineral interests in a property. The Operator may keep the leases in their office and not record them until they have all of the signatures they need. In this way they avoid divulging to any competitors that they are pursuing a particular tract of land.

Do you have a Surveyor's plat of the land tract(s)? The Operator may not have this yet but it would be nice to see. They will have to have a professional Surveyor's plat with the location of the proposed well at the time that they apply for a drilling permit at the state regulatory agency. The County Tax Assessor's Office may have a plat of the property. The U.S. Geological Survey is an excellent source of professional topographic maps that will allow you to assess the topography of the area. Their maps are free. You just have to search for them on the usgs.gov web site.

Has the Operator applied for a drilling permit? The Operator may not have applied for a drilling permit at the time they are talking to you but it is a good question to ask. If they have applied for a permit then the Surveyor's plat showing the lease and the well's proposed locations should be available.

Are the adjacent tracts of land leased by other Operators? This lets you know if you will be interacting with competitive Operators or if you will be in an area by yourself - at least initially. If there are offset Operators (Competitive Operators on adjacent tracts of land) then it is possible that you will at some time in the future enter in to a race to deplete a certain reservoir if there is a reservoir that truly extends across the lease line. Fluid flow across a lease line can be detected by observing the pressure behavior in two or more wells. If two wells are in the same reservoir, then pressure depletion in one well will ultimately be detected in the second well. If there is an offset Operator that has a waterflood in progress then you may benefit from or be harmed by those operations. Be careful. And finally there is the implied covenant to protect a lease from drainage by offset Operators. The implied covenant to protect a lease from drainage is a part of oil and gas law that requires an Operator to drill wells on their lease if a "Prudent Operator" would deem it necessary to protect the lease from being drained by the wells of a competitive Operator on an adjacent tract of land. This is something to be aware of from the beginning. Some oil and gas leases, like the one in the chapter in this book about oil and gas leases, include a clause that allows the Operator to release any portion of the leased premises at any time. Such a release could be used to eliminate such an obligation.

Is the lease accessible by public roads? You hope the answer is yes. If not, you may need or want easements to travel across the surrounding property. You will also want to know if the Operator will need any special permission to move the drilling rig on the public roads nearby. Some roads require permits for large over-weight vehicles.

Are there any small bridges that must be crossed along any dirt roads (public or private) on the way to the proposed well site? If so, will a very heavy drilling rig be able to cross those bridges given their weight restrictions? Are there any height restrictions such as low over passes or electric wires that will prevent a drilling rig from being brought to the location? Drilling contractors are familiar with all of these road-related issues because they have to move their rigs constantly. The odds are high that a drilling contractor can get a rig to your location, but it is best to think it through just in case your location has an exceptional condition. You will want workover rigs and oil tanker trucks to have access to the lease throughout the life of the well.

Has the location been known to flood after certain weather events? If the land floods or becomes extremely muddy during drilling operations it will only slow your progress and add to your intangible costs. Muddy areas will also be an impediment to workover rigs and production personnel in the future. But on the up side, dirt and mud locations cost less than caliche, gravel, shell, or boards and they are easier to fully restore in the event of a dry hole.

Will vehicles be able to drive to the location un-aided after a heavy rain or snow; or will they need to be towed with a bull dozer? Adding bull dozer towing will add to your expenses. If you will be drilling on a dirt location during a rainy season, you may want to include bull dozer costs in your AFE. Every truck may have to be towed in and out of the location. Bring your rubber boots!

❓For the depth of the well that will be drilled, what spacing requirements have been set by the state's regulatory agency?

❓For the depth of the well that will be drilled, what is the minimum distance that a well can be staked relative to the nearest lease line, and what is the minimum distance between wells?

❓Will we meet those requirements or will we have to seek an exception? All of these questions determine how many wells you will be able to drill on a lease and where you will be able to stake them.

❓Is all of the land within the leased premises available for oil and gas drilling or are certain parts designated as off limits in the lease? There may be restrictions against drilling within a certain distance of a house, barn, or water well. The same holds true for seismic operations and these restrictions can leave gaps in your seismic data.

❓Where will the well or wells be located within the tract?

❓Is the site where the well will be drilled a naturally flat area or will it need to be built up?

❓Are there row crops on the property? At what time of year are there growing crops in the field? This will affect your surface damages.

❓What else is the property used for? Cattle, hunting, mining?

❓Is the location near a city, town, or other populated place? If so, there will be more liabilities in the event of a blowout.

❓Do you plan to conduct geophysical operations on the lease and/or the surrounding property?

❓Will you acquire 2-D or 3-D seismic data?

❓Does the Operator have permission to conduct geophysical operations on the property? How was this permission obtained? It may be in an oil and gas lease or in a separate seismic agreement with the land owner.

❓What geophysical contractor will acquire the data and when?

❓Will the geophysical contractor use single-component geophones or three-component geophones?

❓Will the geophysical contractor use vibroseis trucks, an accelerated weight drop, or buried dynamite?

- Will the geophysical contractor need to use bull dozers to clear any brush or other vegetation?

- When will the data be available from the geophysical contractor?

- Who will have ownership and unlimited access to the geophysical data after it is acquired?

- Who will have the authority to sell the seismic data in the future?

- Will I as an investor have access to the seismic data after the partnership has terminated?

- Who will interpret the seismic data?

- Will the interpreter be looking for structures or amplitude anomalies? What kind?

Does the Operator have all necessary permits for conducting geophysical operations on the surrounding properties if necessary? It may be nessesary to shoot seismic tails on part of the surrounding property to get the best possible seismic data on your own lease.

Is there any existing seismic data in the area that can be purchased? There are seismic data brokers that sell seismic data owned by others.

# Chapter 18 Questions about the Well

Where will the well be staked? The Operator will have to have a professional Surveyor's plat with the location of the proposed well at the time that they apply for a drilling permit at the state regulatory agency. The County Tax Assessor's Office may have a plat of the property.

Do you have a topographic map of the area? Are there any surface obstructions such as lakes, rivers, buildings, dams, airports, or roads? Are any areas described as off-limits in the lease such as areas near existing buildings?

Have you located the previously drilled wells in the area? You might want to do this to make sure that what you find in the field matches your paper records. Old wells that have been plugged and abandoned can often be found with a metal detector. You can dig down a few feet with a shovel to confirm your find.

Where will we get water for the drilling fluid? Will we drill a water well, take water from a pond, or haul it to location? Will there be a cost associated with using surface water?

If we are using surface water from a lake, pond, or river, will we use it to mix the cement? If so, have we tested the water's ion and dissolved solids content? Water that is high in chlorides can cause the cement to set too quickly.

If a water well will be drilled, how deep will it be drilled; how much will it cost; and how much water will it produce per hour?

Will the water well be left for the surface rights owner to use? Often the answer is yes.

What kind of location will be built? And who will build the location? How much will it cost? How long will it take? Some of the possibilities include dirt, calichie, bull rock, shell, or a boarded location. If a boarded location is used, the boards may be rented. What kind of roads will be built? Dirt roads, calichie roads, shell?

Will it be necessary to install a gate or a cattle guard?

❓Will the rig use earthen pits or metal tanks to hold the drilling fluid?

❓Is there sufficient room for a gas flare?

❓If the well is a successful oil well, where will the oil stock tanks be located? The tanks may be near the well or a pipeline may be laid to an area beside a public road so that trucks can easily pull up to the tanks to load oil or produced water.

❓If the well is a successful oil well, who will purchase the oil and how will it be transported from the lease? Will it be by truck or pipeline? Has pricing been negotiated with the purchaser?
Oil purchasers are registered with the state regulatory agencies.

If the well is a successful oil well, is electricity available in the area to power a pump jack or will it be necessary to use a propane tank for fuel? Will gas from the production stream be used?

If the well is a successful gas well, what nearby pipeline will the Operator connect to? What is the pressure in that pipeline? Does the Operator have all necessary easements to lay pipe from the wellhead to the receiving pipeline? What is the connection cost and what are the sales terms? You should be able to see pipeline markers (small signs) on the ground where these pipelines intersect public roads or travel along the side of public roads.

Is the land level in the location where the wells are projected to be drilled? Will the site need to be built up with a bull dozer to make it level?

What kind of drilling rig will be used: a single, a double, or a triple? A “single” is a drilling rig that is capable of pulling one joint of drill pipe out of the hole at a time and racking back a stand of one joint in the derrick. Such a stand is roughly 30 feet tall. A “double” is a drilling rig that is capable of pulling two joints of drill pipe out of the hole at a time and racking back a stand that consists of two joints in the derrick. Such a stand is roughly 60 feet tall. A “triple” is a drilling rig that is capable of pulling three joints of drill pipe out of the hole at a time and racking back a stand that consists of three joints of drill pipe in the derrick. Such a stand is roughly 90 feet tall. Larger drilling rigs usually also have a higher lifting capacity and are thus able to drill to deeper depths. So singles are used for shallow wells. Doubles are used for wells of intermediate depth. And triples are used for deeper wells.

- Will the rig be on a day rate or a turnkey contract?

- If the rig will be on day rate, who will be on location to represent the Operator?

- Will conductor pipe be set? If so, what size and how deep?

- Will the well be a straight hole or deviated? If deviated, will the well be horizontal?

- If it will be a deviated well, will you be using a bent sub or rotary steerables?

- Do the MWD contractors have experience in that area in that formation?

- How deep will surface casing be set?

- What size of surface casing will be set?

- Will it be necessary to run intermediate casing? If so what size will it be and how much will it cost?

- What size production casing will be set if the well is successful?

- What bit sizes will be used in each section of the well?

- What kind of drill bits will be used in each section of the well: Tri-cone or PDC?

- Will the drill bits be rented or purchased?

- What kind of drilling fluid will be used in each section of the well? Fresh mud or oil base mud?

- Will a Mud Engineer be on location to monitor the drilling mud?

- What mud weights are expected to be required?

- Is the fracture gradient known?

- Can a kick be detected at the surface? If so, how?

- What kind of BOP will be used?

- How will the BOP's be tested?

- How will the casing shoes be tested?

- Will the well penetrate any over-pressured or depleted zones?

- Will the temperature of the mud returns be monitored?

- Will a Mud Logger be on location?

- Will the Mud Logger have a gas chromatograph?

- Will the Mud Logger save samples?

- Will Logging-While-Drilling (LWD) be used?

❓What indications on the electric logs will determine that a well is successful or unsuccessful?

❓Will the Operator run any high-tech electric wireline logs such as 3-D resistivity, elemental composition, magnetic resonance, borehole imaging, or multipole acoustics?

❓Will the Operator take wireline or LWD fluid samples?

❓Will the Operator take whole cores or sidewall cores or no cores?

❓How will the fluid samples and cores be used to evaluate the commercial capacity of the well?

❓Who will perform the formation evaluation at the casing point?

❓Will I as an investor receive copies of the electric logs, mud logs, fluid sampling and pressure testing reports, core analyses, seismic products, morning reports, mud reports, and Driller's Reports? You should. Preferably by email at the same time that everyone else receives them.

❓If the well is deviated, will any special procedures be used to mitigate operational risk during the wireline operation?

❓Will the production casing be set in tension to avoid buckling? The answer should be yes.

❓How will the pay zone be completed?

❓How will the well be perforated?

❓Will the pay zone be stimulated? Will it be by hydraulic fracturing, acidizing, or other means?

Who will design the hydraulic fracture treatment?

Will the designer of the hydraulic fracture treatment have the rock mechanics properties they need such as Poisson's Ratio and Young's Modulus? If not, will the Operator run a multipole acoustic logging tool so that those parameters can be obtained?

Can substantial advantages be gained in the hydraulic fracture treatment design by drilling a larger borehole or by using larger diameter tubulars?

How will the well be tested?

What methods of artificial lift will be used and how much will they cost to install and operate? Will they be used throughout the life of the well or will they need to be changed as the production changes?

What surface equipment items are likely to be needed? How much will they cost to purchase and install?

Will you purchase new or used production equipment?

# Chapter 19 Legal Questions

Are the oil and gas leases recorded in the county courthouse?

Have I, as the potential investor, read the oil and gas lease myself? The Land Man's run sheets and copies of the relevant documents in the county records along with the attorney's title opinion letter give you as much comfort as possible that the Lessors do indeed own 100% of the Mineral Interest; but only by reading the oil and gas lease that you can see exactly what interests and what rights they have conveyed.

Have any overriding royalty interests been assigned by the Lessee?

Are any overriding royalty interests going to be assigned by the Lessee?

Is a Geologist being compensated with an overriding royalty interest? If so, what is the percentage?

Is a Geophysicist being compensated with an overriding royalty interest? If so, what is the percentage?

Is a Land Man being compensated with an overriding royalty interest? If so, what is the percentage?

Is an Attorney being compensated with an overriding royalty interest? If so, what is the percentage?

Is anyone else being compensated with

an overriding royalty interest? If so, what is the percentage?

What is the net revenue interest for the lease(s)? Net Revenue Interest (NRI) is 100% minus the mineral interest royalty (stated in the oil and gas lease) minus all overriding royalty interests assigned by the Lessee of an oil and gas lease. The net revenue interest is typically 75-80% but it can be more or less.

What are the state and local severance and ad valorem tax rates for this location?

Are the mineral interest owners and overriding royalty interest owners paying their pro rata share of state and local severance taxes and ad valorem taxes? Is this arrangement explicitly stated in the oil and gas lease?

How much time remains in the primary term of the lease(s)?

Have you run title all the way back to sovereignty? Have you seen the run sheets?

Do you have a title opinion letter for each oil and gas lease?

Does the mineral rights owner also own the surface rights or have the mineral rights been severed?

Will the Operator have to pay for surface damages? If so, how much?

Is there a provision for surface damages in the lease?

# Chapter 20 Financial Questions

Do you have a pro-forma cash flow statement?

What revenue and cost assumptions were used to make these calculations?

What risk factors were used?

How might these revenues and costs vary?

What is the Return on Investment (ROI)?

What is the Discounted Cash Flow Rate of Return (DCFROR) also known as Internal Rate of Return (IRR)?

What is the Net Present Value at a 10% Discount (NPV)?

# Glossary

**Abstract Number** - The land in every County in Texas is broken up in to parcels called abstracts and every abstract has an abstract number. Parcels of land within a county in Texas may be identified by their abstract number. A parcel of land with an abstract number of 500 is often expressed in writing as A-500. The land within a particular abstract may be entirely owned by one party or it may be subdivided in to smaller tracts of land that are each owned by one or more parties.

**Abstract of Title** - The history of ownership of a tract of land. It may include all of the title conveyance documents associated with the property going all the way back to sovereignty (the time when the land was owned by the state).

**Acidizing** - An operation in which a strong acid such as Hydrochloric Acid (HCl) is pumped down a wellbore, through perforations in the casing, and in to a formation. The purpose of the operation is to dissolve calcite near the wellbore and in fractures that connect to the wellbore so that oil and gas can flow in to the well bore at higher rates. Acidizing is usually performed in limestone formations or in other formations that contain a significant amount of calcite. Acidizing operations may be performed immediately after perforating a newly drilled well or at any time during the productive life of a well.

**Acre** - A unit of measurement of land area. The amount of land area in an oil and gas lease is usually measured in acres. An acre is 43,560 square feet. A square mile contains 640 acres. The most common drilling and spacing unit required by the Texas Railroad Commission to drill a shallow oil

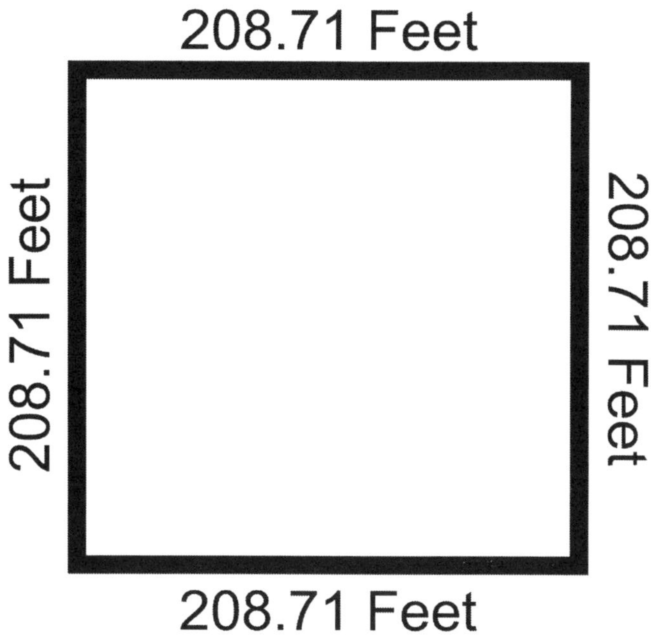


1 Acre
43,560 Square Feet

well is 40 acres. A 40-acre square is 1,320 feet along each side.

**Ad Coelum** - The common law doctrine that a property owner owns everything on their property from the blue sky all the way to the core of the Earth. This doctrine is still observed with respect to solid minerals but it has been replaced by the "Rule of Capture" for fugacious minerals including oil and gas.

**AFE** - Also known as an Authorization For Expenditure, an AFE is a document, usually prepared by an Operator to be presented to non-operating working interest owners in a petroleum property that describes a proposed operation, estimated costs of the operation, and an economic justification for the operation. By submitting an AFE to the non-operating working interest owners, an Operator intends to gain their approval to conduct the proposed operation and their agreement to pay their proportionate costs of the operation.

**Annulus** - The annulus is the space between two concentric cylinders within a wellbore. While a well is being drilled, the annulus is the space between the outside edge of the drill pipe and the borehole wall. In a completed well, the tubing-casing annulus is the space between the outside edge of the tubing and the interior wall of the casing. An annulus also exists between the outside surface of production casing and the inside surface of larger diameter intermediate casing. The annulus is sometime referred to as the "back side".

**Anticline** - An anticline is a subsurface structure resembling an upside down bowl. An anticline is one of the simplest structures for trapping hydrocarbons. As hydrocarbons migrate up dip, they accumulate in the top of the anticline.

**An anticline exposed at the surface.**

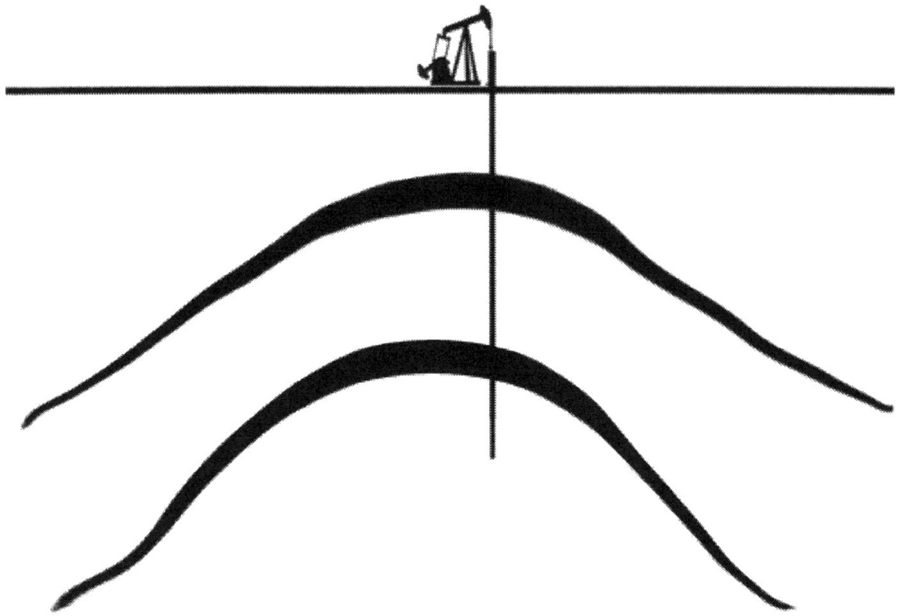

**An anticline trap.**

Thus the tops of anticlines are ideal places to drill oil and gas wells.

**API** - The American Petroleum Institute is an oil and gas industry organization that sets standards for oil and gas equipment, recommends certain operating practices, contributes to safety, and publishes documents to aid policy makers. Visit www.api.org

**API Gravity** - A measure of the density of oil in degrees.
API Gravity = (141.5/Specific Gravity of the Oil at 60 degrees F) - 131.5
Crude oils with an API gravity of 35-50 degrees are light crude oils. Crude oils with an API gravity of 20-35 degrees are medium crude oils. And crude oils with an API gravity of 10-20 degrees are considered heavy crudes.

**API Number** - Since the 1970's, most wells drilled in the United States have been assigned a unique identification number at the time they were drilled called an API number. The first two digits of the number are determined by the state where the well is located. The next three digits are determined by the county that the well is located in. And the final five digits are unique to each individual well.

**A pump jack raises and lowers sucker rods in the wellbore. The sucker rods actuate a pump at the bottom of the well that pushes oil to the surface. Sucker rod lift is a form of artificial lift.**

**Artificial Lift** - When the reservoir pressure is not sufficient to push oil and gas from the reservoir all the way to the surface, fluids will not flow to the surface naturally. They may rise to some level within the well but they will not reach the surface. In cases such as this the Operator will use one of several methods of lifting the liquids to the surface. These methods include rod pumps with pump jacks at the surface, gas lift, and electric submersible pumps.

**Authorization For Expenditure** - Also known as an AFE. This is a document, usually prepared by an Operator to be presented to non-operating working interest owners in a petroleum property that describes a proposed operation, estimated costs of the operation, and an economic justification for the operation. By submitting an AFE to the non-operating working interest owners, an Operator intends to gain their approval to conduct the proposed operation and their agreement to pay their proportionate costs of the operation.

**Back In** - The right to receive an interest in a petroleum property in the future if certain contractually specified conditions are met. The interest that a party may obtain from a Back In is known as a reversionary interest.

**Back In After Pay Out** - A particular kind of Back In where a party such as an Independent Geologist, Deal Finder, or Investment Promoter receives a working interest in a petroleum property (a well or group of wells) after it has produced enough money to pay back the initial costs of drilling and completing the well or wells to the working interest owners who paid those expenses. Back in after payout is sometimes abbreviated as (BIAPO).

**Barrel** - A barrel is a unit of volume equal to 42 gallons. Oil quantities are most often measured in barrels. A barrel is abbreviated as "bbl" or "BBL" or sometime "BO" which means barrels of oil. A barrel is equal to 5.6145833 cubic feet.

**Basement** - The "Basement" is igneous rock of Pre-Cambrian age that underlies Phanerozoic sedimentary rock throughout most of the world. It is usually granite. Most sedimentary rocks in the world are of Paleozoic, Mesozoic, or Cenozoic age - which means they are 0 to 542 million years old. Rocks created more the 542 million years ago were formed during a period of Earth's history known as the Pre-Cambrian time. They tend to be non-sedimentary rocks such as granite and they rarely contain oil and gas. Thus, drilling operations usually cease when a well bore penetrates all of the younger rocks that were deposited between zero and 542 million years ago and then enters the "Basement" which is more than 542 million years old. Experience and conventional thinking says that there is very little to be gained from drilling in the "Basement".

**Basin** - A basin is a natural depression in the Earth's surface resulting from tectonic activity. A basin is many miles or kilometers in width. Over many millions of years sediments from rocks in higher positions around the basin are eroded and grains are transported by water, wind, or glaciers in to the basin. After these layers of sediments accumulate and are gradually buried by subsequent sediments, they are later lithified to form sedimentary rock. Hydrocarbons may later migrate up through the rock and become trapped in certain local structures or simply within certain permeable strata. It is for this reason that basins full of sedimentary rock are target areas for oil and gas exploration. Hundreds of basins have been identified throughout the world. The largest oil and gas producing basin in the lower 48 states is the Permian Basin which is filled with sediments of Paleozoic age.

**BCF** - Billion Cubic Feet. A BCF is a unit of measurement of natural gas volume meaning one billion cubic feet of gas at standard conditions of 1 atmosphere of pressure and 60 degrees Fahrenheit. If natural gas is selling for $5.00 per thousand cubic feet (MCF), then one million cubic feet (MMCF) is worth $5,000.00 and one billion cubic feet (BCF) is worth $5 million.

**Behind Pipe** - A term that refers to oil and gas reserves in a particular formation that is accessible within an existing wellbore where casing has been set, but where no attempt has yet been made to perforate the casing at the depth of that formation to produce those reserves of oil and gas. Such reserves of oil and gas are said to be "behind pipe". If a well is drilled and multiple pay zones are encountered and production casing is run. The Operator will usually begin by producing the deepest pay zone first and then moving up the well and producing each additional pay zone one-by-one. In such a case while the deepest zone is being produced first. All of the other zones would be described as reserves "Behind Pipe".

**Blue Sky Laws** - State laws relating to the sale of securities such as interests in an oil well. Blue Sky Laws are designed to protect the assets of financially uneducated and inexperienced persons.

**Bonus** - A sum of money paid by the Lessee (Oil Company) to a Lessor (Mineral Interest Owner) as an incentive and as good and valuable consideration at the time an oil and gas lease is executed (signed) by a Lessor. The amount is negotiable and is often based on a certain number of dollars per acre of land being leased.

**Borehole** - The hole or pathway created by drilling a well in to the ground.

**BS & W** - Base settlement and water. When crude oil is brought to the surface and stored in an oil stock tank, a small amount of water and solids will usually accumulate on the bottom of the tank because the oil is not completely pure.

The BS&W has no economic value and its volume, if any, is excluded when calculating the amount payable when oil is sold from one party to another.

**Calcite** - The mineral calcium carbonate Ca $CO_3$. Calcite is the primary component of limestone. It can also exist as cement in a sandstone formation. Calcite fizzes with bubbles when drops of hydrochloric acid (HCL) are placed on it. This is a means of distinguishing calcite from dolomite which does not fizz.

**Caliper Log** - A log that measures the diameter of the inside of a wellbore at various depths. It is usually a continuous series of measurements that are three to six inches apart within a well over a planned interval that can be thousands of feet in length. Caliper logging tools may have a single arm that produces a simple one-dimensional measurement or they may have many arms extending from the tool that measure in multiple azimuths and create a three-dimensional image of the borehole wall. Caliper logs can be run in open hole or cased hole. Drillers often use caliper logs to calculate the amount of cement they must pump behind the casing when they run a string of casing in open hole. Production Engineers sometimes use caliper logs in cased holes to identify wear on the inside of the casing. Caliper logs can be acquired with both mechanical fingers and acoustic travel time measurements.

**Carried Interest** - Also called a "carry". A carried interest is an interest that is converted to a working interest if and when certain previously negotiated conditions are met. When the conversion occurs, the existing working interest owners jointly and proportionately surrender a portion of their working interest to create room for the new working interest that is owned by the new party. The owner of a carried interest does not receive revenue from that interest and is not liable for costs associated with the interest until the time that the carried interest is converted to a working interest. The three most common conditions or times when a carried interest is converted to a working interest are (1) when a well has been drilled to the casing point, (2) when a well has been drilled and casing and surface facilities have been set and the well is about to begin production ("A Carried Interest Through the Tanks"), and (3) at the time the costs of drilling and completing a well have been recouped by the initial working interest owners or investors. This point in time is also known as "Pay Out" or "Project Pay Out". This third arrangement is known as a Back In After Pay Out (BIAPO). After the conversion of a carried interest to a working interest occurs, all parties pay their proportionate share of all expenses going forward. The parties are said to be proceeding "Heads Up" which means no one is being carried and everyone is paying their proportionate share of expenses and receiving their proportionate share of the Net Revenue Interest (NRI).

**Cased Hole** - A well where casing has been run. The opposite of a cased hole is an open hole. An open hole is a borehole where casing has not been run.

**Casing** - Pipe, usually made of steel, that is inserted along the entire length of a borehole to preserve the borehole and prevent collapse or cave-in of the surrounding rock. It also prevents unwanted fluids from entering the well from depths above or below the pay zones. Casing must be designed to withstand internal bursting pressure, external collapse pressure and the tension resulting from the buoyed weight of all of the casing hanging below each joint. The American Petroleum Institute (www.api.org) has developed design standards for casing. These provide standard diameters and standardized strengths.

**Casing**

Casing and tubing are described by their outside diameter (OD), weight per foot, and API metal grade such as J-55, L-80, N-80, or P-110. The thicker the casing wall, the smaller the inside diameter (ID) and the higher the weight per foot. Common casing diameters range from 2-7/8 inches to 13-3/8 inches. Casing strings are designed from the bottom up with safety factors for burst, collapse, and tension. Casing should be set in tension at the surface in order to prevent buckling down hole. Most casing comes from the mill in joints that are approximately 40 feet in length.

**Casing Point** - The point in time when a well has been drilled to its planned total depth and the working interest owners must decide whether to run production casing and complete the well or to plug and abandon the well as a dry hole.

**Christmas Tree** - A visible assembly of valves and fittings on the surface at the top of a well that is used to control the flow of produced liquids and gases. It also provides the well's Operator with access to the production tubing.

**Christmas Tree**

**Circulating** - Pumping drilling fluid down the inside of drill pipe, casing, or tubing and back up to the surface through the annulus. When an Operator is drilling a well using a rotary rig, the

Operator is almost always circulating while drilling. The flow of drilling fluid down the inside of the drill pipe, through jets in the drill bit and then back up the annulus serves several purposes. First, it cools the drill bit. Second, it clears the chunks of rock that the bit cuts (called cuttings) from the surface where the drill bit is cutting so that the drill bit can efficiently continue to drill ahead. And third, the circulating drilling fluid lifts the cuttings to the surface so that the borehole is clear. The cuttings are removed from the drilling fluid on the surface by passing the fluid across a shale shaker.

Note: It is at or near the shale shaker where Mud Loggers obtain their cutting samples.

Circulating may also be performed in a cased hole wherein completion fluid is pumped down the inside of tubing and then back up the tubing-casing annulus.

**Circulating System**

A circulating system is an integral part of every rotary drilling rig. It consists of a mud pit or mud tanks, pumps, a stand pipe in the derrick, a mud hose connecting the stand pipe to the top of the kelly, the drill string, shale shakers, and sometimes a mud gas separator.

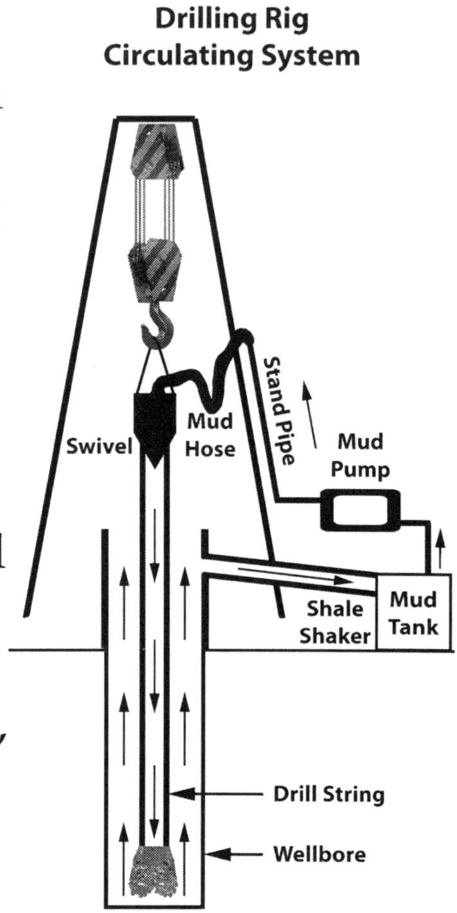


**Circulating Bottoms Up** - Circulating for a sufficient period of time to allow the drilling fluid that is at the bottom of the wellbore at the time the Operator begins circulating to be returned to the surface. An Operator will often "Circulate Bottoms Up" when they have drilled a well to its planned depth but before beginning to trip out of the hole with the drill pipe and drill bit. This is one last effort to clean the wellbore and remove any cuttings or mud balls before tripping out of the hole to run wireline logs and then casing.

**Completion** - All of the operations that are conducted in a well after a well has been drilled and evaluated and a decision has been made to attempt to produce oil and gas from the well. Completion operations prepare a well to begin producing. Completions includes such operations as perforating, stimulating the well by hydraulic fracturing, acidizing, running downhole equipment such as tubing, plugs, packers, sucker rods, pumps, and other artificial lift equipment.

**Condensate** - Also known as distillate. Condensates are hydrocarbons that exist in a gaseous phase while in the reservoir at natural reservoir temperature and pressure but later condense in to a liquid phase when they are brought to the surface where pressures and temperatures are lower. Changes in temperature and pressure can occur as these hydrocarbons are traveling up the wellbore toward the surface and when they are on the surface. Condensed liquids are usually low in density and relatively clear or transparent in appearance. A condensate gas reservoir is a gas reservoir that contains some hydrocarbons that will condense in to liquid phase when brought to the surface and allowed to assume lower pressures and temperatures. Condensate is very valuable. An Operator will take steps to insure that condensate is captured at the surface and sold.

**Core Sample** - A core sample is a sample of rock from a subsurface formation. Core samples or "cores" may be obtained in three ways. The first method involves using a cylindrical shaped drill bit called a core bit that has a rough cutting surface around its bottom edge and cylindrical hole in its center. It is attached to the bottom of the drill string in lieu of a standard bit. As the core bit rotates it cuts a cylindrically shaped hole in the rock and leaves a smaller segment of rock in the center untouched. The core bit swallows the rock in the center and that rock is later brought to surface. A similar feat could be achieved by thrusting the open end of a drinking straw in to mashed potatoes and then withdrawing the straw. You would obtain a "core sample" of mashed potatoes inside the straw. Core samples from a well are usually 3-6 inches in diameter and can be tens to hundreds of feet in length. A core sample obtained in this way is called a whole core. Coring in this way is perhaps the best means of formation evaluation because you can see the rock, its grains, its pores, its composition, its post-depositional history, and the pore fluids.

If you are searching for oil you can place the core samples under a fluorescent light and those cores that contain oil will fluoresce and appear bright yellow like a yellow highlighter pen. They may also smell like oil! The Bureau of Economic Geology in Texas has huge facilities in Houston, Austin, and Midland that store over 2 million boxes of core samples that have been recovered from thousands of wells in Texas. The facilities are open to the public so you can visit these facilities and view any of these core samples.

Smaller core samples can also be obtained using wireline tools. There are two types. Rotary sidewall coring tools which use a tiny core bit and an electric motor that drills and recovers cores from the side of a wellbore.

And finally percussion sidewall coring tools use a propellant to force small metal cups into the side of a wellbore. The cups are then pulled out of the rock using a pair of cables. Percussion sidewall coring is the least expensive of the three methods. The jarring action makes the cores unsuitable for permeability measurements but they are very useful for quickly determining whether or not a particular zone contains oil and gas or not.

**Crude Oil** - Also known as crude. Crude oil is a natural mixture of liquid hydrocarbons as it exists underground and when it is brought to the surface. Crude oil is oil that has not been processed in a refinery. Crude oil varies widely in its composition and its physical properties of color, density, and viscosity. Crude oils contain alkanes, naphthenes, and aromatic hydrocarbons. If a crude oil is designated as sweet it means that it does not contain $H_2S$. If a crude oil is described as sour it means that it contains appreciable amounts of $H_2S$. Sweet crude is preferable because it costs less to refine. Futures contracts for crude oil are traded in the CME Group.

**Cuttings** - Small pieces of rock produced by the cutting action of a drill bit as it drills through a formation. Cuttings are cleared from the rock face beneath the drill bit and lifted to the surface by the circulation of drilling fluid down the inside to the drill pipe and back up the annulus. The annulus is the space between the borehole wall and the outside of the drill pipe. Cuttings are removed from the drilling fluid at the surface using a device called a shale shaker. A Mud Logger analyzes cuttings recovered at the surface for lithology and the presence of oil, water, and gas.

**Day Work Drilling Contract** - A contractual arrangement between an Operator and a Drilling Contractor where the Operator directs the Drilling Contractor in the drilling of a well and the Operator pays the Drilling Contractor an agreed fixed amount per day.

**Delay Rental** - A payment made by the Lessee (Oil Company) to the Lessor (Mineral Rights Owner) of an oil and gas lease that extends the primary term of the lease and thus extends the time that the Lessee has available to begin drilling on the lease premises. A "Paid Up Lease" is an oil and gas lease that does not include provisions for Delay Rentals. In a "Paid Up Lease" the primary term is set at the time the lease is executed and no delay rental payments are ever required.

**Depletion** - The normal process of removing oil and gas from a reservoir. When a reservoir is depleted there is less oil and gas remaining in the ground and the reservoir pressures are often less than they were before the well or wells were drilled. However, in the case of water drive oil or gas reservoirs the reservoir pressure may remain relatively constant as the oil and gas are depleted because the water moves in to fill the void left by the hydrocarbons that are produced.

**Depletion Allowance** - The lawfully prescribed deduction of a certain percentage of an Operator's production when calculating U.S. federal income taxes due from oil and gas production operations. This tax benefit of oil and gas investing flows through to working interest owners including investors in oil and gas wells. The depletion allowance for small oil companies is currently 15%. The democrat party in the United States eternally seeks to remove this deduction while the Republican Party eternally defends it.

**Dip** - The angle of a layer of sedimentary rock relative to horizontal. Horizontal layers of rock are said to have a dip of zero degrees. If beds were thrusted to a point that they were completely vertical they would have a dip of 90 degrees. Most underground formations are somewhere in between. While most sedimentary rock is deposited in horizontal layers those layers can be

tilted later as a result of tectonic activity. Dip is important to Oil and Gas Operators because oil floats on water and gas floats on oil. If oil, gas, and water are present in permeable layers of rock, and the rock is tilted or is dipping in one direction, the oil and gas will naturally migrate "up dip" to the higher end of the rock because oil and gas float on water. Operators are often trying to determine which direction is up dip of existing productions so they can drill more wells. Moving down dip would increase the odds of drilling in a portion of the rock that is completely saturated with water rather than oil and gas. You can observe this same phenomenon by filling a bottle half-and-half with oil and water and then holding the bottle horizontally but slightly tilted. The oil will accumulate in the higher end of the bottle and the water will accumulate in the lower end of the bottle.

**Dip Log** - A dip log is a wireline log or LWD log that measures the dip of the formations that surround a wellbore. Dip log tools often have six arms that extend radially from the tool with pads on them that detect the formations as they pass by. There are also three-dimensional resistivity logging tools that can measure formation dip without touching the borehole wall. These can be useful in rugose (rough) or washed out boreholes. Knowing the dip of a pay zone can suggest which direction to go to drill the next well. Dip logs can also be used to gain clues about the structures of the formations that a well penetrates.

**Directional Drilling** - Directional drilling means intentionally drilling a wellbore that is not vertical. This includes deviated wells and horizontal wells. An Operator may drill a deviated (non-vertical) well for several reasons. First, the Operator is unable to position a drilling rig directly above the target because of an obstruction on surface such as a lake, river, airport, or building. Second, an Operator may want to drill a well through two or more subsurface targets that do not lie directly above and below each another. A directional well would be required to drill through those targets. And finally an Operator may wish to drill horizontally. This may be done to maximize production rates by maximizing the surface area of the pay zone that is exposed to the wellbore or to maximize the number of natural fractures in a pay zone that are penetrated by a wellbore. The trajectory of a directional well can be monitored and controlled while it is being drilled through the use of MWD tools (Measurement While Drilling tools).

**Division Order** - A division order is a document that lists all of the people and entities that have an interest in a well and their numerical interest. The list includes mineral interest owners, overriding royalty interest owners, and working interest owners. A division order directs the payment of proceeds from the sale of produced products to the appropriate parties in the correct percentages.

**Downhole** Anything that exists or occurs within a wellbore below the surface of the Earth is downhole.

**Drill Bit** - The device attached to the bottom of the drill string that is used to crush and scrape rock to create a borehole. Rotary Drill bits are available in two broad groups: rolling cutter and drag bits.

The most common roller cutter bits are tri-cone rolling cutter bits. Tri-cone rolling cutter bits have three rolling cones with teeth mounted on them that roll on the rock face at the bottom of the wellbore to crush, grind, and scrape the rock.

**Tri-Cone Rolling Cutter Drill Bit**

Drag Bits have no moving parts. They have fixed blades finished with extremely strong metal alloys such as tungsten carbide that scrape the rock as the bit turns. Sometimes the blades have industrial diamonds inserted along their edges that assist in tearing the rock as the bit turns. The number of blades on a drag bit ranges from two to seven. The choice of a drill bit depends on the kind of rock that is expected and the amount of footage that the Operator intends to drill through. A drill bit may be purchased from a bit manufacturer or rented. If rented, the price is usually for an agreed amount per foot that the drill bit is used to drill.

**Polycrystalline Diamond Compact Bit (PDC Bit)**

**Drill Pipe** - Metal pipe that is used to drill a well. Drill pipe is specially made for the purpose of turning the drill bit. It connects the drilling rig at the surface to the drill bit that is turning at the bottom of the well. Each section of drill pipe is called a joint of drill pipe or simply a joint. Each joint is approximately 30 feet long. Joints of drill pipe are threaded with a male connection on one end and a female connection on the other end so that they can be connected in a string of pipe thousands of feet in length. A

**Joints of drill pipe on a pipe rack.**

long string of drill pipe connected end to end in a well is called a drill string. Drill pipe is hollow so that drilling fluid can be pumped down the inside of the pipe, through the bit, and back up the annulus to the surface. The male end is called the pin and the female end is called the box. Drill pipe usually has a greater wall thickness than tubing and casing because it is subjected to abusive torque, vibration, compression, and tension during drilling operations. This is especially true when drill pipe is beginning to stick or is stuck. Drill pipe ranges in diameter from 3-1/2 inches to 6-1/2 inches. A drilling rig that is tall enough to pull two 30-foot joints of drill pipe (60 feet) at a time and stand them back in the derrick is called a "Double". A drilling rig that is tall enough to pull three 30-foot joints of drill pipe (90 ft) at a time and stand them back in the derrick is called a "Triple".

**Drill String** - Joints of drill pipe are threaded with a male connection on one end and a female connection on the other end so that they can be connected in a string of pipe thousands of feet in length. The string of drill pipe connected end to end in a well while it is being drilled is called the drill string. The drill string connects the drill bit to the drilling rig.

Rotating the drill string causes the bit to rotate.

**Drilling Break** - A sudden increase in the rate of penetration of the rock while drilling. A drilling break is experienced whenever the bit encounters a layer of rock that is easier to drill through. This can be a layer of rock with higher porosity and or higher pore pressure. If it is layer of higher porosity, then it may also be a pay zone; but a drilling break by itself does not mean that the bit has encountered a pay zone.

**Drilling Rig** - The equipment that is used to drill an oil and gas well. A rotary drilling rig consists of a hoisting system, a circulating system, and a rotary system. The hoisting system includes the substructure, derrick, crown block, traveling block, elevators, hook, and drawworks. The circulating system includes the mud pits or tanks, pumps, stand pipe, mud hose, swivel, drill string and shale shaker. The rotary system includes the kelly, kelly bushing, rotary table, drill pipe, drill collars, and drill bit. For more information about drilling rigs read the chapter about drilling a well.

**Dry Gas** - Gas that does not contain any significant amount of hydrocarbons that will condense in to a liquid phase if the pressure and or temperature of the gas are decreased. Dry gas is almost entirely composed of methane ($CH_4$).

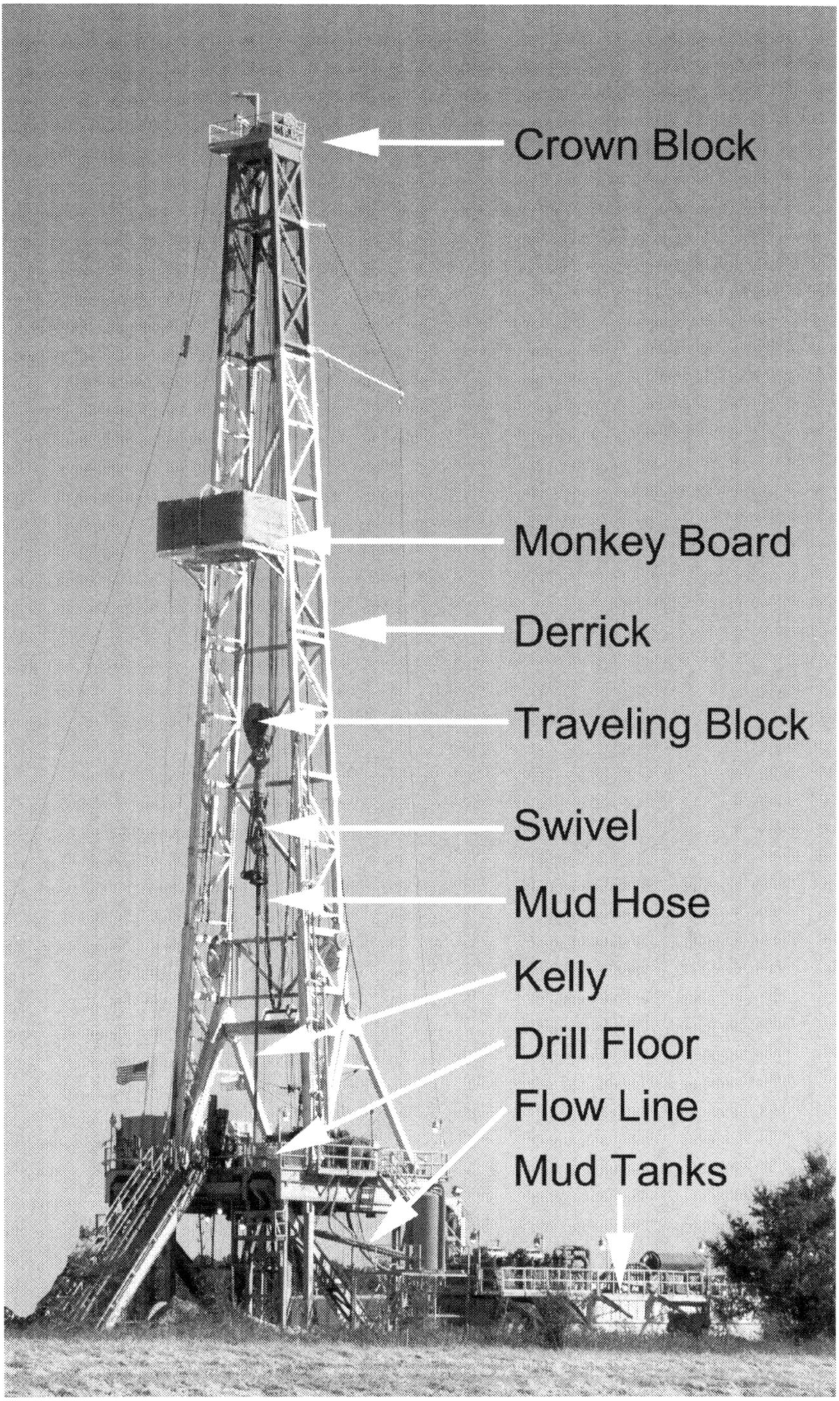


**Rotary Drilling Rig**

**Dual Completion** - An arrangement of equipment within a wellbore that enables the well to produce oil and gas from two different pay zones simultaneously. The production from the pay zones are kept separate from one another by producing them through two different paths within the wellbore that are isolated from each other. Dual completions are more complex than single completions but they allow the Operator to enjoy the time value of money benefit of producing two zones at the same time.

**Estimated Ultimate Recovery** - An estimate of the total amount of oil and gas that a well will produce over its entire lifetime from when it is drilled through the day that it is plugged and abandoned. The ultimate recovery of a well may be estimated by performing a decline curve analysis of the production history of the well and by analyzing the ultimate recoveries of nearby analogous wells. Multiplying the estimated ultimate recoveries of oil and gas by assumed product sales prices for each barrel of oil and each mcf of gas provides a potential investor with an estimate of the total revenue that a well will yield over its lifetime. For example, a shallow oil well that produces 50,000 barrels of oil over its lifetime of five years will yield a gross revenue of $4,000,000 if the average price received for each barrel sold is $80. If that well can be drilled and evaluated for $250,000 and completed for an additional $250,000 it may represent an attractive investment for some investors.

**Farm Out** - An agreement where a party that holds the leasehold interest in an oil and gas lease (Lessee and Farmor) agrees to assign an interest in that Lease to another party (the Farmee) with the expectation that the Farmee will commence drilling operations on the lease and the Farmor will gain a benefit such as a retained interest in any successful wells that are drilled.

**Fault** - A fracture or crack through sedimentary rock where the rock layers on one side of the fracture have moved up, down, or sideways relative to the rock layers on the other side of the fracture.

**A fault exposed at the surface with two different kinds of rock on each side of the fault plane.**

During tectonic convergence, rocks may be compressed to the point that a fault forms and some rock layers are pushed up and over other rock layers that they were formerly beside. This kind of fault is called a reverse fault. The side of the fault where the rock layers have moved up relative to the other side is called the up-thrown side. The side of the fault where the rock layers have moved down relative to the other side is called the down-thrown side.

During tectonic extension or separation, rocks may be pulled apart in such a way that a fault forms and some rock layers slide down and away from the other rock layers that they were formerly beside. This kind of fault is called a normal fault. Normal faults form when continental plates are moving away from each other. The side of the fault where the rock layers have moved down relative to the other side is called the down-thrown side of the normal fault. The higher side is called the up-thrown side.

**Fee Ownership** - In the oil and gas industry fee ownership usually means ownership of all interests in a property including mineral interests and surface rights. Hence, a fee interest owner may drill a well on their property without needing an oil and gas lease. There is a second and far less common meaning to the term "fee interest" in property law where "fee interest" means that the interest may be passed from one generation to another generation.

**FINRA** - The Financial Industry Regulatory Authority (FINRA) is the largest independent regulator for all securities firms doing business in the United States. FINRA seeks to protect America's investors by insuring that the securities industry operates fairly and honestly. FINRA oversees nearly 4,700 brokerage firms, about 167,000 branch offices, and approximately 637,000 registered securities representatives.

**Fishing** - An operation where an Operator is attempting to locate and retrieve any article that has been lost or left in a well. Such operations are known to be costly and time-consuming. A very wide range of tools are employed to latch on to items that are lost or left in a well. These are called fishing tools. The item an Operator is attempting to recover is called "the fish" regardless of what it is.

**Folding** - The bending of sedimentary rock layers in response to tectonic forces.

**Formation** - A layer of sedimentary

**Folded rock formations.**

rock. Its properties and characteristics are distinguishable from the layers of sedimentary rock above and below it.

**Fracture** - A crack in a formation. It may be natural or it may be the result of a hydraulic fracture stimulation. Unlike a fault, the rock on either side of the crack need not move relative to the rock on the other side for the opening to be considered a fracture.

**Gamma Ray** - Gamma rays are high-frequency short-wavelength electromagnetic radiation emitted from the nuclei of atoms. Gamma rays are continuously released in nature by certain isotopes of potassium, uranium, and thorium. One of the most common logging tools in the oil and gas industry is a gamma ray logging tool. A gamma ray tool counts the number of naturally emitted gamma rays produced by subsurface formations around the wellbore that are detected within a one-second time interval at the detector of the tool that is in the wellbore. Shales tend to contain more potassium than sandstones or carbonates. So higher gamma ray counts within a particular formation tend to indicate a higher percentage of shale. Formations with low gamma ray counts are called "clean" formations and these are most likely to be non-shales such as sandstones and carbonates. Gamma ray measurements are usually made every three to six inches for the entire length of a logged interval - which can be thousands of feet. Some gamma ray tools are capable of not only counting the number of gamma rays detected at the tool but also distinguishing the energy level of each gamma ray. This allows a Log Analyst to determine what elemental isotope emitted each gamma ray whether it was potassium, uranium, or thorium. These tools are called spectral gamma ray tools. Most gamma rays in most wells are emitted by potassium in shale. However, uranium and thorium sometimes appear in subsurface formations in high concentrations. Gamma rays emitted by uranium or thorium are not related to shale content and their presence can skew an analysis if their gamma rays are inadvertently assumed to be from shale. Gamma ray tools function in both open hole and cased hole. This fact allows cased hole tools such as perforating guns to be set in a well "on depth" with or "correlated" with specific zones seen on open hole logs that also included a gamma ray tool.

**Gas** - Also known as natural gas. A mixture of hydrocarbons that occur naturally in underground reservoirs in a gaseous phase or state. Natural gas composition is usually limited to varying amounts of methane ($CH_4$), ethane ($C_2H_6$), propane ($C_3H_8$), butane ($C_4H_{10}$), carbon dioxide ($CO_2$), oxygen ($O_2$), nitrogen ($N_2$), and hydrogen sulfide ($H_2S$). Though not all natural gases contain all of these molecules. Natural gas may also contain trace amounts of Helium, Neon, and Xenon. The term "dry gas" means a composition of natural gas that is almost entirely methane. "Wet gas" is a natural gas mixture that contains 80-90% methane with the remainder of the molecules including the natural gas liquids of ethane ($C_2H_6$), propane ($C_3H_8$), butane ($C_4H_{10}$) and some larger alkanes.

**Gas Cap** – A gas cap is an accumulation of gas above a zone of liquid oil or water in a porous layer of rock. A similar but much smaller gas cap can be found at the top of every bottle of soda before it is opened. If a gas cap exists above an oil zone, the Operator may initially attempt to produce only the oil and avoid producing gas from the gas cap so that the gas cap stays intact and pushes down on the oil for as long as possible and provides the pressure support that is necessary to recover as much oil as is possible. After the oil is produced, and there is no longer a need for the gas cap to push down on the oil, the gas in the gas cap can be produced.

**Gas Cap Drive Oil Reservoir** - In a gas cap drive oil reservoir, there is large gas reservoir immediately above and in communication with the oil reservoir. The pressure of the gas is exerted down against the oil. The pressure from the gas above the oil pressurizes the oil to equal the gas's pressure at the gas-oil interface. When the wellbore is perforated in the oil zone, the gas in the gas cap begins to push the oil toward the wellbore. If the wellbore perforations are made only in the oil zone and far below the gas cap, the initial production may be at or near 100% oil. Over time some of the gas will begin to form a cone that extends down through the oil zone toward the perforations. Eventually some of this gas will "break-through" and be seen in the produced fluid along with the oil. From that point forward, the production will include both oil and gas. This is an undesirable circumstance because the production of gas from the gas cap will cause the pressure in the gas cap to decline and thus exert less pressure on the oil reservoir. As less pressure is exerted on the oil, the oil production rate decreases and the amount of oil that can ultimately be recovered is reduced. So when an Operator knows that an oil reservoir's drive mechanism is a gas cap, they will perforate wellbores only in the oil zone so that gas from the gas cap is not produced; and thus the pressure in the gas cap is kept as high as possible for as long as possible while oil is being produced.

**Gas-Oil Ratio (GOR)** - The ratio of produced gas to produced oil in a producing well measured in mcf of gas per barrel of oil.

**Geologic Time Scale -** The Earth is approximately 4.5 billion years old.

Geologists have divided up that time in to smaller blocks of time and given those blocks of time names for ease of communication and called it the Geologic Time Scale. The largest blocks of time are Eons. Eons are divided in to Eras. Eras are further divided into Periods. Periods are divided in to Epochs. Epochs are divided into Ages. The most recent 542 million years of Earth's history are of the most interest to Petroleum Geologists because most life on Earth has lived during that time and it is in rocks of this Eon where most organic matter exists and where most oil and gas reservoirs are found.

**Geophone** - A small device consisting of a coil of wire and a magnet hanging from a spring inside the coil of wire. Geophones are placed on the ground in seismic surveying operations to sense the movement of the ground up and down as compressional waves from the seismic source reflect off of layers of rock in the subsurface. As they travel back to the surface they cause an up and down oscillation of the ground. As the ground moves up and down, the coil inside the geophone moves up and down with the ground. But the magnet that is hanging from the spring does not move up and down as much as the coil of wire because it is hanging from a spring. So there is relative movement between the coil and the magnet as the ground moves up and down. This creates an alternating magnetic field around the magnet. As a result of the alternating magnetic field, the coil of wire outputs a small alternating voltage with a magnitude that varies directly with the velocity of the coil relative to the magnet. This alternating voltage of approximately 0.5 volts at its maximum is passed through amplifiers, noise filters, and analog to digital converters and recorded in a computer. The graphs of these output voltages of the geophones versus time constitute traces of seismic data.

**Geophysicist** - A Geophysicist is a person who uses their understanding of geophysical principles to study and describe the geology of the Earth. Geophysicists study seismic data to define prospective drilling locations. Visit the Society of Exploration Geophysicists at www.seg.org

**Gravity** - Also known as API Gravity. A measure of the density of oil in degrees.

API Gravity = (141.5/Specific Gravity of the Oil at 60 degrees F) - 131.5

**HBP** - Held by Production. When a property is Held By Production, it means that the property is leased under the terms of an oil and gas lease and remains unavailable to be leased by other oil companies because at least one well on the property is producing oil and or gas.

**Held By Production** - Also known as HBP. When a property is Held By

Production, it means that the property is leased under the terms of an oil and gas lease and remains unavailable to be leased by other oil companies because at least one well on the property is producing oil and or gas.

**Horizontal Drilling** - A form of directional drilling where an Operator intentionally and gradually deviates the trajectory of a well from vertical at the surface to horizontal at some deeper depth and then continues to drill horizontally - usually through a pay zone. An operator may drill a long section of the wellbore horizontally to maximize production rates and ultimate recovery by maximizing the surface area of the pay zone that is exposed to the wellbore; or with the intent to maximize the number of natural fractures in a pay zone that are penetrated by a wellbore. Many Operators drill horizontal wells in shale plays throughout the U.S.

**Hydrocarbons** - Organic compounds composed of the elements of hydrogen (H) and carbon (C). There are three major groups of hydrocarbons: alkanes, naphthenes, and aromatics.

The chemical formula of the first group of hydrocarbons, called alkanes, is $C_nH_{2n+2}$ where n represents a varying number of carbon atoms in the molecules. Alkanes are chains of carbon atoms surrounded by hydrogen atoms. Common hydrocarbons that are of interest in the petroleum industry are the first eight members of the alkanes group: methane ($CH_4$), ethane ($C_2H_6$), propane ($C_3H_8$), butane ($C_4H_{10}$), pentane ($C_5H_{12}$), hexane ($C_5H_{14}$), heptane ($C_7H_{16}$), and octane ($C_8H_{18}$).

Alkane molecules with more than 20 carbon atoms are waxy solids at surface temperature and pressure. They are called paraffins.

Hydrocarbon molecules also form in rings with the chemical formula of $C_nH_{2n}$. These are called naphthenes.

Benzene is a ring-shaped molecule that has the chemical formula of $C_6H_6$. To meet the valence requirements, a benzene ring includes three single bonds and three double bonds between the Carbon atoms. The benzene ring is the foundation of the group of hydrocarbons called aromatic hydrocarbons.

**Initial Potential** - Also known as IP. The initial potential is the initial flow rate of oil or gas that a newly completed zone is determined to be capable of producing at as a result of a test. Newly completed zones are almost always tested soon after they are completed to determine their initial potential. The information obtained from the test is submitted to the state regulatory agency on a standard form. There is one form for oil wells and another form for gas wells.

**Independent Oil Company** - Any oil and gas exploration and production company that is not one of the major international oil companies and does not have refining operations. If you directly invest in an oil well, you will almost certainly be investing in a well that will be operated by an Independent Oil Company.

For more information about independent oil companies, visit the Independent Petroleum Association of America at www.ipaa.org

**Intangible Drilling Costs** - Also known as IDC's. Intangible drilling costs are all of the costs of drilling and completing a well that do not include the purchase of any tangible item. Intangible drilling costs include all expenditures that have no salvage value. Casing, tubing, and surface production equipment may be salvageable after a well has finished producing and thus they are not included in intangible drilling costs.

The classification of every expenditure during the drilling and completion of a well as either intangible or tangible is important because federal tax law allows Operators and Investors to write off 100% of all intangible costs during the year that those expenses are incurred. Tangible costs must be capitalized and depreciated. Most of the costs of drilling and evaluating the productive capacity of a well are intangible drilling costs. Running production casing in a successful well is one of the first significant tangible costs.

**Joint** - Each individual section of drill pipe, casing, or tubing that is threaded on both ends is called a joint. Joints of drill pipe and joints of tubing are both approximately 30 feet long. Joints of casing are approximately 40 feet long. A drilling rig that is tall enough to pull two 30-foot joints of drill pipe (60 feet) at a time and stand them back in the derrick is called a "Double". A drilling rig that is tall enough to pull three 30-foot joints of drill pipe (90 ft) at a time and stand them back in the derrick is called a "Triple".

**Joint Operating Agreement** - Also known as a "J.O.A." A Joint Operating Agreement is a contract between the working interest owners of a petroleum property that describes how they will jointly develop and operate the property. It is an essential part of any direct oil and gas investment. There are two versions of JOA's that are widely used. They were promulgated by the American Association of Petroleum Land Men during the 1980's and they are still in use today. They are the A.A.P.L. Form 610-1982 Model Form Operating Agreement and the A.A.P.L. Form 610-1989 Model Form Operating Agreement. These documents were preceded by the A.A.P.L. 1956 Form and the A.A.P.L. 1977 Form.

**Kelly and Kelly Bushing** - A kelly (also known as a kelly joint) is special piece of pipe at the very top of the drill string that is square or hexagonal in cross-section. A kelly bushing is a device seated in the rotary table of the drilling rig that clenches the flat surfaces of the kelly and rotates the kelly. Rotating the kelly rotates the drill pipe below it and in turn rotates the drill bit. The kelly bushing turns the kelly similar to the way a wrench turns a nut. The kelly joint is free to move up and down through a hole in the kelly bushing. As the drill bit drills deeper the drill string moves down into the hole and the kelly moves down through the kelly bushing.

**Land Man** - A person who locates the owners of mineral interests in parcels of land and negotiates oil and gas leases for those parcels of land on behalf of an oil company. Land Men also work to cure defects in title. A Land Man may be male or female. Visit the American Association of Professional Land Men which has approximately 12,000 members at www.landman.org.

**Lease** - Also known as an oil and gas lease. An oil and gas lease is a written contract wherein a mineral interest owner, known as the Lessor, grants the right to explore for oil, natural gas, and other hydrocarbons to an oil company or other entity, known as the Lessee, for a specific period of time. An oil and gas lease is both a conveyance and a contract. It conveys certain mineral rights and establishes conditions which the Lessee must meet during the term of the lease. An oil and gas lease is considered a "Deed with the Possibility of Reverter" which means the interest may revert to the Lessor when the lease expires. For much more information see the chapter in this book about oil and gas leases.

**Limestone** - A sedimentary rock composed primarily of the mineral calcium carbonate. During the Paleozoic Era vast shallow seas covered much of North America and especially Texas. Marine life was abundant in these warm shallow seas. Shallow sea plants and animals including corals, echinoderms, anthozoans, bryozoans, algae, brachiopods, bivalves, cephalopods, gastropods, graptolites, and arthropods such as trilobites flourished in the warm waters. Some of these organisms such as corals and algae secreted calcium carbonate as part of their biologic processes during their life. Many of the other organisms retained calcium carbonate in their bodies, shells, and skeletons. Calcium carbonate sediments from both living and dead organisms built up on the sea floor over millions of years to form layers of limestone that are now thousands of feet thick. Many of these limestone formations hold millions of barrels of oil and billions of cubic feet of natural gas.

**Logging** - An operation where instruments with special sensors are lowered in to a well to measure certain electrical, physical, and nuclear properties of the rock strata surrounding the wellbore. The measurements are then analyzed to determine which formations contain commercial quantities of oil and gas and which do not. Logging tools can be

**Electric Wireline Logging Operation**

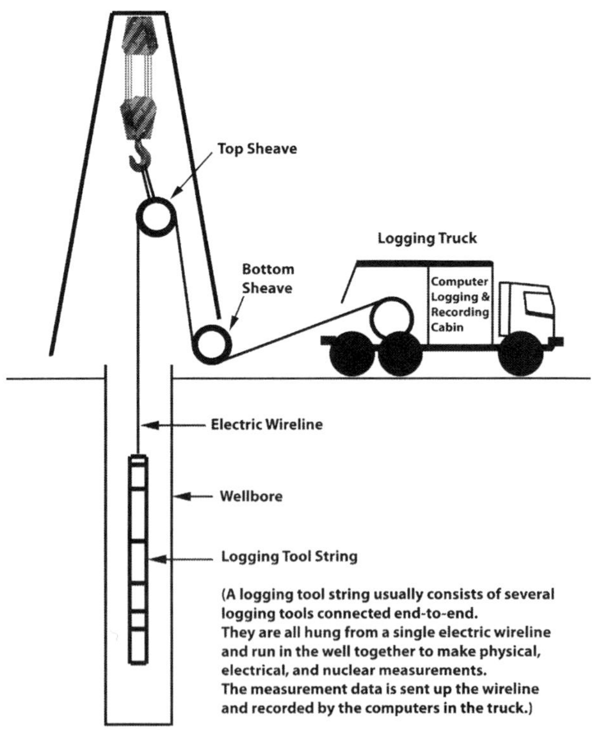

conveyed in to and out of a wellbore on electric wireline or drill pipe. Some logging tools function only in open hole. Others function only in cased holes. The professionals who analyze log data are called Petrophysicists or Log Analysts.

For more, visit the Society of Petrophysicists and Well Log Analysts at www.spwla.org. They have local chapters throughout the world.

**MCF** - The most common unit of measurement of volume of natural gas in the United States. One MCF or mcf means one thousand cubic feet of natural gas at standard conditions of one atmosphere of pressure and 60 degrees Fahrenheit. Similarly, one MMCF or mmcf means 1,000 mcf or one million cubic feet of natural gas at standard conditions of one atmosphere of pressure and 60 degrees Fahrenheit.

**Measured Depth** - Abbreviated as MD, the measured depth of a well or a point in a well bore is the depth of that point from the surface as measured along the axis of the borehole. The true vertical depth of a well or a point in a wellbore is the depth as measured from that point directly to the surface along an imaginary vertical line that is perpendicular to the surface and extends through the point, regardless of whether or not the wellbore follows such a perfectly vertical line.

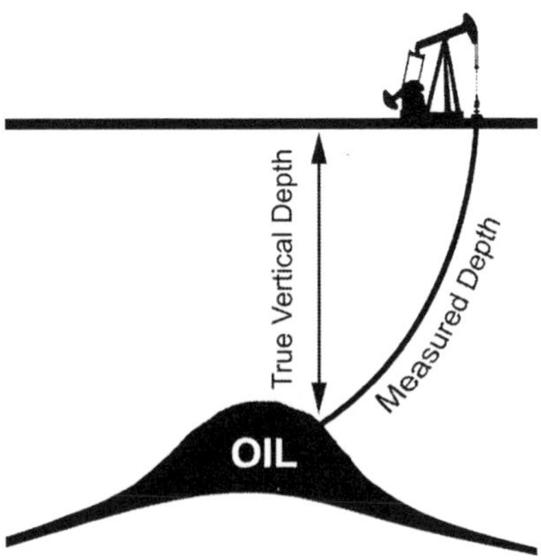


Measured Depth
and True Vertical Depth

**Measurement While Drilling (MWD)** - A technology that an Operators uses to monitor and control the deviation and directional azimuth (compass direction) of a wellbore while it is being drilled. MWD tools have evolved to include LWD tools which means Logging While Drilling. In addition to monitoring deviation and azimuth while drilling, it is now possible to acquire log data such as gamma ray, resistivity, porosity, acoustics, and magnetic resonance measurements while drilling. These are LWD tools.

**Mineral Interest** - The right to explore for and produce oil, gas, and other minerals from a parcel of land. The mineral interest is conveyed from the mineral interest owner to the Lessee in an oil and gas lease.

**Mother Hubbard Clause** - A "Mother Hubbard" clause in an oil and gas lease is often included in the granting clause. It acts to include all land owned by the Lessor, if any, that are adjacent to and contiguous with the land in the legal description so that the lease covers all land owned by the Lessor in that location, regardless of whether the legal description perfectly describes the boundaries of the land. In this way, no small slivers of land are inadvertently left out of the lease.

**Mud** - Also known as drilling mud or drilling fluid. Mud is continuously circulated down the inside of the drill pipe, through the bit, and back up to the surface in the annulus while drilling operations are in progress. The mud serves several purposes. First, it provides a means of transporting the cuttings to the surface. Second, it provides the hydrostatic pressure that is necessary to offset the pore pressure of the fluids in the pores of the rock formations that the well is penetrating. If this hydrostatic pressure is not present or not sufficient, the well will blow out. And third, the mud cools and lubricates the drill bit as it turns. A Mud Engineer is an expert in the chemical and mechanical properties of drilling mud. A Mud Engineer may design a drilling fluid before a well is drilled and then frequently monitor the composition and properties of the actual drilling fluid while a well is being drilled. They can make adjustments as necessary. A Mud Report describing the composition and properties of the mud is usually produced at least once per day while a well is being drilled.

**Mud Logger** - This person analyzes cuttings recovered at the surface for lithology and the presence of oil, water, and gas. Some Mud Loggers also monitor the composition of the gas. Cuttings are small pieces of rock produced by the cutting action of a drill bit as it drills through a formation. Cuttings are cleared from the rock face beneath the drill bit and lifted to the surface by the circulation of drilling fluid down the inside of the drill pipe and back up the annulus. The annulus is the space between the borehole wall and the outside of the drill pipe. Cuttings are removed from the drilling fluid at the surface in a device called a shale shaker.

**Natural Gas -** A mixture of hydrocarbons that occurs naturally in underground reservoirs in a gaseous phase. Natural gas composition is usually limited to varying amounts of methane ($CH_4$), ethane ($C_2H_6$), propane ($C_3H_8$), butane ($C_4H_{10}$), carbon dioxide ($CO_2$), oxygen ($O_2$), nitrogen ($N_2$), and hydrogen sulfide ($H_2S$). Though not all natural gases contain all of these molecules. Natural gas may also contain trace amounts of Helium, Neon, and Xenon. The term "dry gas" means a composition of natural gas that is almost entirely methane. "Wet gas" is a natural gas mixture that contains 80-90% methane with the remainder of the molecules being the natural gas liquids of ethane ($C_2H_6$), propane ($C_3H_8$), butane ($C_4H_{10}$) and some larger alkanes.

**Net Revenue Interest (NRI)** - The net revenue interest is the revenue interest held in a petroleum property by the working interest owners after the burdens of mineral interest royalty and overriding royalties are subtracted. For example, if an oil company leases a property with a 15% mineral interest royalty, and a 1% overriding royalty interest for the Land Man, then the Net Revenue Interest is 84%.

**Normal Fault** - A normal fault is a fault where the block of rock above the fault plane (the hanging wall) moves downward along the fault plane relative to the other block (the foot wall). A normal fault results from formations that are in tension. Normal faults are most likely to form when tectonic plates are moving apart or separating from one another.

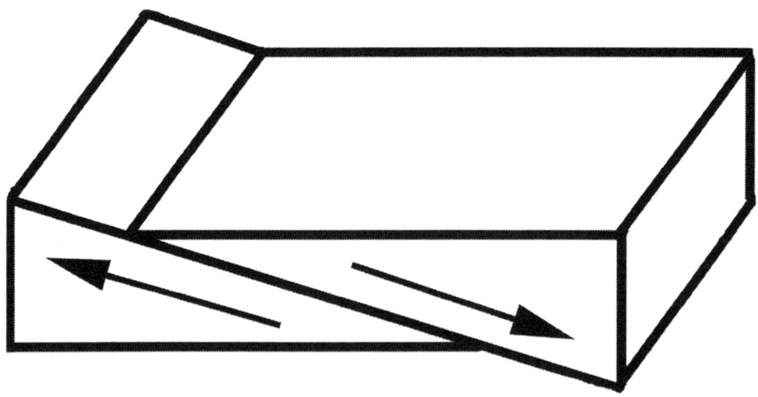

Normal Fault

**Oil and Gas Lease** - Also known simply as a lease. An oil and gas lease is a written contract wherein a mineral interest owner, known as the Lessor, grants the right to explore for oil, natural gas, and other hydrocarbons to an oil company or other entity, known as the Lessee, for a specific period of time. An oil and gas lease is both a conveyance and a contract. It conveys certain mineral rights and establishes conditions which the Lessee must meet during the term of the lease. An oil and gas lease is considered a "Deed with the Possibility of Reverter" which means the interest may revert to the Lessor when the lease expires. For much more information see the chapter in this book about oil and gas leases.

**Open Hole** - A section or interval of a wellbore where casing has not been run.

**Operator** - The working interest owner that is responsible for drilling, completion, production, workovers, lease management, accounting, and regulatory compliance for a petroleum property. The responsibilities of the Operator are enumerated in the Joint Operating Agreement (JOA).

**Outcrop** - A place where an underground rock formation breaches the surface and is thus visible. Outcrops provide Geoscientists with rare opportunities to study rock formations that usually buried and thus impossible to see.

**An outcrop in Azerbaijan.**

**Overriding Royalty** - Also known as an overriding royalty interest or ORRI or simply an override. An overriding royalty interest is a revenue interest in a petroleum property that is created by assignment from the working interest owner. Like a mineral interest owner's royalty, it entitles the owner to a percentage of the revenue from the property free of the costs of production but net of state taxes. An overriding royalty interest expires when the underlying oil and gas lease expires. Overriding royalty interests are often assigned by working interest owners to professionals such as Geologists, Geophysicists, Land Men, and Attorneys who contribute to the initial creation of an oil and gas project in lieu of or in addition to cash compensation.

**Packer** - A downhole tool that serves to block or plug the annulus either in cased hole or open hole.

**Paid Up Lease** - An oil and gas lease that does not have a provision for delay rentals. A paid-up lease is in effect from the day it is executed through the end of the primary term without the need for any delay rental payments.

**Pay Zone** - The sedimentary rock formation that contain commercial quantities of producible hydrocarbons.

**Pay Out** - The point in time in an oil and gas project when the working interest owners have recouped their initial exploration and development costs from the net proceeds of the sale of produced hydrocarbons.

**Percentage Depletion** - Depletion provides for the recovery of capital investment over time. Percentage depletion is a tax deduction that is calculated by applying an allowable percentage to the gross income from a property. For oil and natural gas the allowable percentage is 15 percent. This effectively means that 15% of a petroleum property's revenue from product sales is tax free.

Federal tax law limits the use of the 15% percentage depletion deduction of oil and gas in several ways. First, the percentage depletion allowance may only be taken by independent producers and royalty owners and not by integrated oil companies. Second, depletion may only be claimed up to production levels of 1,000 barrels per day of oil or 6,000 mcf per day of natural gas. Third, the deduction is limited to 65% of net taxable income. Fourth, the net income limitation requires percentage depletion to be calculated on a property-by-property basis. It prohibits percentage depletion to the extent that it exceeds the net income from an individual property. These limitations apply both for regular and alternative minimum tax purposes. Percentage depletion in excess of the

65 percent limit may be carried over to future years until it is fully utilized.

**Perforating** - An operation where a device is lowered in to a well either on electric wireline or pipe and positioned within a pay zone and activated. The result is the creation of holes in the casing and the surrounding cement that extend in to the formation. Oil and gas can then flow from the formation, through the holes in the casing, and in to the wellbore. There are a wide assortment perforating units in various shapes and sizes for various applications. The performances of the various units can be modeled prior to a perforating job to aid in selection.

**Permeability** - A measure of a rock's natural capacity to allow fluid to flow through it. Higher permeabilities are desirable because they allow for higher production rates and higher cumulative production if all other factors are constant. Permeability usually increases with increasing porosity. Increasing compaction, poorly sorted grains, and the presence of any form of cementation within the pore space all serve to decrease permeability. Approximations of permeability can be made using downhole formation testing tools and also with magnetic resonance devices.

**Petroleum** – Petroleum is a complex mixture of hydrocarbons.
Hydrocarbons are molecules that are primarily composed of the chemical elements of Hydrogen (H) and Carbon (C). In nature, atoms of these two elements are combined in an infinite number of ways to create many different hydrocarbon molecules.
The simplest hydrocarbon molecule is methane. It contains a single carbon atom and four hydrogen atoms. Carbon has a valence of four and hydrogen has a valence of one. So hydrocarbon molecules tend to form structures that

satisfy these valence numbers. All of the alkanes satisfy these requirements. The chemical formula of alkanes is $C_nH_{2n+2}$ where n represents the number of carbon atoms in the molecule. Common hydrocarbons of the alkane group that are of interest in the petroleum industry are the first eight members of the alkanes group: methane ($CH_4$), ethane ($C_2H_6$), propane ($C_3H_8$), butane ($C_4H_{10}$), pentane ($C_5H_{12}$), hexane ($C_6H_{14}$), heptane ($C_7H_{16}$), and octane ($C_8H_{18}$). Alkane molecules with more than 20 carbon atoms are waxy solids at surface temperature and pressure. They are called paraffins. They can precipitate out of a liquid oil production stream in the wellbore and in surface equipment. Aside from alkanes, hydrocarbon molecules also form in rings with the chemical formula of $C_nH_{2n}$. These are called naphthenes. Benzene is another ring-shaped molecule that has the chemical formula of $C_6H_6$. A benzene ring includes three single bonds and

three double bonds. Benzene forms the foundation of a group of hydrocarbons called aromatic hydrocarbons. Crude oil contains thousands of different molecules of alkanes, naphthenes, and aromatic hydrocarbons.
Petroleum is a complex mixture of hydrocarbons that may contain these and other hydrocarbons in varying compositions and proportions.

The term "Petroleum" includes both liquid crude oil and natural gas and mixtures of the two. Crude oil composition varies. So its color, density, viscosity, and commercial value also vary. Crude oil can be clear, green, brown, yellowish, black, and all phases of color in between. The density varies from half of the density of water to denser than water. It can flow easily or resist flow with viscosities much like honey or tar. Its viscosity can also vary with temperature. Other compounds are sometimes mixed with the petroleum such as $CO_2$, $H_2S$, Nitrogen, and saline water. Petroleum that contains $H_2S$ is dangerous because $H_2S$ is a poisonous gas and it can be costly because it speeds the corrosion of metal equipment that it contacts such as casing and tubing. Crude oil that contains $H_2S$ is referred to as sour crude. Alkanes can readily be separated from one another in a refinery and then sold in nearly pure form or used to create mixed products such as gasoline, diesel, and heating oil. For more information read the chapter about petroleum.

**Petroleum Engineer** - An Engineer who specializes in oil and gas exploration and production. Petroleum Engineering is further subdivided in to the three areas of Drilling, Production Engineering, and Reservoir Engineering. Many universities offer BS, MS, and PhD degrees in Petroleum Engineering. The Society of Petroleum Engineers (SPE) has tens of thousands of members worldwide.

**Petroleum Geologist** - A Geologist who specializes in oil and gas exploration and production. Many universities offer BS, MS, and PhD degrees in Petroleum Geology. The American Association of Petroleum Geologists (AAPG) has tens of thousands of members worldwide.

**Plug and Abandon a Well** - Also known as "Plugging and Abandoning" or P & A. This is the finally operation to permanently close a well. A well is permanently closed or abandoned for two primary reasons. First, when a new well is drilled and evaluated and found to be incapable of producing in paying quantities then it will be immediately plugged and abandoned. Such a well is known as a "Dry Hole". The "plugging" portion of the term "plug and abandon" refers to a part of the operation where cement is pumped into several sections of the wellbore to form permanent plugs so that fluids will not be able to travel up or down inside the well after it is abandoned. The cost of plugging and abandoning a well must be included in the "Dry Hole Cost" of drilling a new well.

The second reason that a well is plugged and abandoned is that it has reached the end of its productive life and it is no longer capable of producing in paying quantities. All oil and gas wells are required to be plugged and abandoned when they are no longer capable of producing oil and gas.

Plugging and abandoning a well involves removing any reusable downhole equipment from within the wellbore including tubing and casing. The next step is to pump cement inside the wellbore at depths specified by the state regulatory agency. And finally the casing is cut off a few feet below ground level and a steel cap is welded on top of it. Then dirt is placed on top of it to make the ground level. If there are no other productive wells on the lease, the Operator will remove surface equipment and surface facilities. A plugging report is submitted by the Operator to the State Regulatory Agency at the time a well is plugged and these reports are available to the public.

**Plug Back** - To block a deeper section of a wellbore where an Operator has been producing from and move up the hole to initiate production in a shallower pay zone. Plugging back is a permanent abandonment of the deeper zone.

**Pooling** - Combining adjacent tracts of land that are under different oil and gas leases to assemble enough contiguous acreage to meet the minimum drilling spacing unit required by the state regulatory agency to obtain a drilling permit. Some oil and gas leases grant the Lessee the right but not the obligation to pool all or any part of the leased premises with any other lands whenever the Lessee deems it necessary.

**Porosity** - The ratio of pore space within a rock to the total volume of the rock. Porosities of oil and gas reservoirs typically range from 5% to 35%. Higher porosities are better than low porosities because higher porosities mean there is more space occupied by oil and gas.

**Primary Term** - The primary term is the period of time designated in the habendum clause in most oil and gas leases during which an Operator is granted the right to begin drilling operations without the obligation to do so. Most oil and gas leases state that the lease shall be in force for a primary term of a specific number of years -- typically one to five years -- from the date that the lease is executed, and for as long thereafter as oil or gas or other substances are produced in paying quantities from the leased premises or from lands pooled or unitized therewith. If the lease is not producing in paying quantities and the Operator is not engaged in continuous drilling operations at the end of the primary term, then the oil and gas lease terminates.

**Prospect** - A geographic area where one or more people believe that commercial quantities of oil and gas may exist underground. The area may be large or small and may be tested by a single well or it can require many wells for appraisal and development. A prospect is a drilling idea that can be bought and sold with or without an oil and gas lease existing at the location.

**Re-Entry** - The operation of opening and entering a wellbore that was previously plugged and abandoned in an effort to restore production in a zone that was previously producing -- or -- initiate production in a zone that had not previously been produced

--or-- to deepen the well to produce hydrocarbons from a zone that is deeper than the total depth of the well.

**Reserves** - The amount of oil or gas available to be produced from one or more reservoirs.

**Reservoir** - A body of porous and permeable rock where hydrocarbons accumulate in commercial quantities and are produced from.

**Resistivity** - A property of a material that describes its resistance to the flow of electricity. Resistivity is one of the primary logging measurements made in oil and gas wells. Resistivity logs can be run on electric wireline or on drill pipe. With the exception of some clays, grains of rock do not conduct electricity. And oil and gas do not conduct electricity. Saline formation water does conduct electricity. So generally speaking, if the salinity of formation water is constant, then the resistivity of a formation is inversely related to porosity. However, if a formation is logged with high porosity and high resistivity, the high resistivity may be indicative of that formation being saturated with oil and gas rather than saline water. The unit of measurement of resistivity is ohm-meters. The inverse of resistivity is conductivity.

**Reverse Fault -** A reverse fault is a fault where the block of rock above the fault plane (the hanging wall) moves upward along the fault plane relative to the other block (the foot wall). A reverse fault occurs when formations are in compression. Reverse faults are most likely to form when tectonic plates are converging.

**Reversionary Interest** - An interest in a petroleum property that becomes effective at a contractually specified date or when certain contractually specified conditions are met.

**Risk** - The possibility of loss associated with an uncertainty. Every investment in the oil and gas industry has risk.

**Roughneck** - A person who works on a drilling rig during drilling operations. A crew of roughnecks is lead by a Driller who controls the hoisting system, rotary system, and pumping system on a drilling rig. Drillers and roughnecks are supervised by a Tool Pusher who is the highest ranking person working for the drilling contractor at a drilling location.

**Royalty** - A share of the proceeds from the sale of oil and gas produced from a petroleum property apart from that of the working interest owners. Royalties include mineral interest owner's royalty which is paid to the land owner or mineral interest owner and overriding royalty which is assigned by working interest owners to professionals such as Geologists, Geophysicists, Land Men, and Attorneys who contribute to the initial creation of an oil and gas project in lieu of or in addition to cash compensation.

**Sandstone** - A sedimentary rock formed by the cementing together and lithification of quartz grains. Quartz grains are composed of mineral silica which has the chemical formula of $SiO_2$. Sandstone is a clastic sedimentary rock which means it consists of individual fragments called clasts that were produced by the weathering of previous rock formations. Sandstone is a common reservoir rock for oil and gas.

**Saturation** - The percentage of the pore space within a formation that is occupied by a particular fluid. Oil saturation (So) is the percentage of the pore space within a formation that is occupied by oil. Gas saturation (Sg) is the percentage of the pore space within a formation that is occupied by gas. Water saturation (Sw) is the percentage of the pore space within a formation that is occupied by water. A formation that contains nothing but water has a water saturation of 100%. The sum of Oil Saturation plus Gas Saturation plus Water Saturation is 1 (100% of the pore space).

**Secondary Term** – The secondary term is the period of time when an oil and gas lease remains in effect after the primary term.

The primary term of an oil and gas lease is the period of time in most oil and gas leases that an Operator is granted to begin drilling operations or lose the lease for failure to do so. Most oil and gas leases state that the lease shall be in force for a primary term of a specific number of years -- typically one to five years - from the date that the lease is executed, and for as long thereafter as oil or gas or other substances are produced in paying quantities. If the lease is not producing in paying quantities and the

Operator is not engaged in continuous drilling operations at the end of the primary term, then the oil and gas lease terminates.

But if the lease is producing oil or gas in paying quantities after the primary term or the Operator is conducting continuous drilling operations after the primary term, the lease remains in effect. This period of time when the lease remains in effect after the primary term is the secondary term.

**Section** - A square mile of land. 640 acres in the shape of a square.

**Securities Act of 1933** - Often referred to as the "Truth in Securities" Law, the Securities Act of 1933 has two basic objectives: To require that investors receive financial and other significant information concerning securities being offered for public sale; and to prohibit deceit, misrepresentations, and other fraud in the sale of securities. The primary means of accomplishing these goals is the disclosure of important financial information through the registering of securities. This information enables investors, not the government, to make informed judgments about whether or not to purchase a company's securities.

In general, the registration forms require (1) a description of the company's properties and business; (2) a description of the security to be offered for sale; (3) information about the management of the company; and (4) financial statements certified by independent Accountants.

Not all offerings of securities must be registered with the Securities and Exchange Commission. Some exemptions from the requirements exist for (1) private offerings to a limited number of persons or institutions; (2) offerings of limited size; (3) intrastate

offerings; and (4) securities of municipal, state, and federal governments. By exempting many small offerings from the registration process, the government seeks to foster capital formation by lowering the cost of offering securities to the public. Here is a link to the full text of the Securities Act of 1933.
http://www.sec.gov/about/laws/sa33.pdf

**Securities Act of 1934** - This Act created the Securities and Exchange Commission and grants it broad authority over all aspects of the securities industry. This includes the power to register, regulate, and oversee brokerage firms, transfer agents, and clearing agencies as well as the nation's self regulatory organizations such as FINRA. Here is a link to the full text of the Securities Act of 1934.
http://www.sec.gov/about/laws/sea34.pdf

**Security** - A "security" includes any [limited partner interest in a limited partnership, share, stock, treasury stock, stock certificate under a voting trust agreement, collateral trust certificate, equipment trust certificate, preorganization certificate or receipt, subscription or reorganization certificate, note, bond, debenture, mortgage certificate or other evidence of indebtedness, any form of commercial paper, certificate**] in or under a [**profit sharing or participation agreement, certificate or any instrument representing any interest in or under an oil, gas, or mining lease, fee or title, or any certificate or instrument representing or secured by an interest in any or all of the capital, property, assets, profits or earnings of any company, investment contract, or any other instrument commonly known as a security], whether similar to those herein referred to or not and regardless of whether the "security" or "securities" are evidenced by a written instrument.

For more information about the regulation of securities, visit the U.S. Securities and Exchange Commission and the State Securities Board in the state where your prospective projects are located.

**Sedimentary Rocks** - Sedimentary rocks are one of three classes of rocks: igneous, sedimentary, and metamorphic. Sedimentary rocks are formed when older rocks are broken down by weathering or biogenic processes, then transported by water, wind, or ice, and finally deposited in layers of sediment. These layers of sediment are later compacted by the weight of further sediment above them. They later harden, or lithify, to form continuous solid rock. Sedimentary rocks may contain a wide array of minerals but the most common minerals are quartz, feldspar, clays, calcite, dolomite, and evaporites. Sedimentary rocks can be divided in to three types: Carbonates, Clastics, and

Precipitates.

Carbonate sedimentary rocks are composed of limestone which is the mineral calcite (Ca $CO_3$). In some cases magnesium enters the rock and replaces half of the calcium and thus changes the calcite to dolomite (Ca $Mg(CO_3)_2$). Carbonate sedimentary rocks are formed from the deposition of the remains of marine organisms or from calcium carbonate produced by the biologic processes of living organisms in shallow or deep seas. These organisms include algae, shells, and single-cell organisms.

Clastic sedimentary rocks are separated in to four groups based on grain size. They are conglomerates, sandstone, siltstone, and mudstone or shale. Shale is a general description for a rock that is deposited in a low energy environment and is composed of varying amounts of hydrous aluminosilicate clays such as kaolinite, illite, and smectite, together with fine-grain silica (silts), calcite, and sometimes organic material known as kerogen. Shales are often found interbedded or mixed with sandstone. Clean sandstone is a term that describes sandstone without shale.

Precipitates, or chemical sedimentary rocks, form when material precipitates from solution and later lithifys into solid rock. The most common examples are evaporates such as salt and gypsum which form in vast thick layers when the water in a sea evaporates.

Most of the oil and gas in the world has been produced from sedimentary rocks. The sedimentary rocks that hold oil and natural gas are usually limestone, dolomite, sandstone, or shale or mixtures of these.

**Seismic Surveying** - An operation where compressional waves from an energy source on the surface are sent down in to the Earth's subsurface. Those compressional waves reflect off of the surfaces of underground formations. Technically speaking there is a reflection any time a compressional wave reaches a

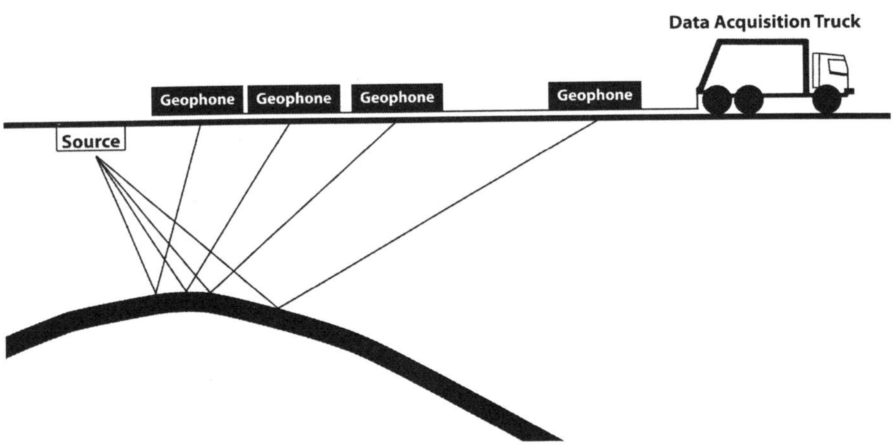


point where there is a change in acoustic impedance. When the reflected waves reach the surface the ground moves up and down in very small increments. The ground movements caused by the arrival of the reflected waves are detected by geophones and the output voltages of the geophones are recorded on computers.

The plots of output voltages from the geophones versus time are later interpreted to determine the structures of subsurface formations and in some cases obtain clues as to the nature of the fluid in the pores of those formations - be they liquid or gas. The energy source on the surface can be a vibroseis truck, an air gun submerged in a pit of water, or dynamite buried approximately 100 feet underground. Vibroseis trucks (also known as vibe trucks) use a very heavy vibrating plate that vibrates against the ground. The vibrations are controlled by the truck. They typically perform a "sweep" of vibrations from a low frequency to a high frequency lasting about 8-10 seconds.

**Separator** - A piece of surface production equipment that separates the oil, gas, and water in a production stream.

**Severance Tax** - A tax paid on the proceeds of produced oil and gas to state and county taxing jurisdictions. Royalty owners are usually responsible for paying the severance taxes on their share of the proceeds from production.

**Shale** - A general description of a clastic sedimentary rock that is deposited in a low energy environment and is composed of varying amounts of hydrous aluminosilicate clays such as kaolinite, illite, and smectite, together with fine-grain silica (silts), sometimes some calcite, and in some cases organic material known as kerogen.

**Shale**

Shales are often found interbedded or mixed with sandstone. Clean sandstone is a term that describes sandstone without shale. Shale can produce oil and gas. The most prominent shale plays in the United States are the Barnett Shale in north Texas, the Haynesville Shale in east Texas and north Louisiana, the Woodford Shale in Oklahoma, the Eagle Ford Shale in south Texas, the Fayetteville Shale in Arkansas, the Bakken Shale in North Dakota, and the Marcellus Shale in the Northeast.

**Shale Shaker** - Also known simply as a "shaker". This is a device on a drilling rig that is used to separate cuttings from the drilling fluid as the drilling fluid returns to the surface during drilling operations.

**Show** - A show is almost anything that is seen during the drilling of a well or on a log that makes someone think there might be oil and gas in a particular zone. A "show" is often seen on a mud log or a wireline log. A show alerts an Operator to pay closer attention to a particular zone. Anyone can declare almost anything to be a show. There is nothing conclusive about seeing or having a "show".

**Shut-In a Well** - To take the physical actions necessary to cause a well to stop producing. It can be as simple as closing a valve.

**Shut-In Royalty** - A special kind of royalty provided in an oil and gas lease that states that if after the primary term one or more wells on the leased premises or lands pooled or unitized therewith are capable of producing oil and gas in paying quantities, but the well or wells are either shut in or production therefrom is not being sold by the Operator, then the Operator will pay a shut-in royalty to the Lessor of a certain number of dollars per acre as specified in the Lease.

**Sidetrack** - A wellbore that branches off of a previously drilled wellbore. Sidetracks are almost never planned prior to spudding a well. They are contingencies that are drilled when the first wellbore either becomes unusable (as a result of equipment being lost in the hole or circulation problems) or does not intersect the desired formation in the desired location. The tool that is used to initiate a sidetrack by diverting a drill bit in to the side of an existing wellbore is called a whipstock.

**Solution Gas Drive Oil Reservoir** - In a solution gas drive reservoir, there is hydrocarbon gas dissolved inside the liquid oil in a reservoir. As oil is produced the pressure of the reservoir declines an some of the dissolved gas comes out of solution and forms small bubbles of gas inside the porespace of the reservoir rock. The pressure from these bubbles pushes the oil toward the wellbore. The gas-oil ratio will increase with time. With all other things being equal, a solution gas drive oil reservoir will yield an ultimate oil recovery that is less than a Water Drive Oil Reservoir.

**Sour Crude Oil** - Also known as "sour crude". Sour crude oil is crude oil that contains significant amounts of hydrogen sulfide ($H_2S$). "Sweet crude" does not have hydrogen sulfide. Sweet crude is preferable to sour crude because it costs less to refine.

**Sour Gas** - Sour gas is natural gas that contains significant amounts of hydrogen sulfide ($H_2S$).

**Source Rock** - A sedimentary rock formation that contains organic material. When the formation is buried under younger sediments and compressed and heated, some of the organic material is converted to oil and gas which later migrates up though the formations above the source rock until it is trapped below an impermeable layer of rock and accumulates to form a reservoir. Shales are often the source rocks for limestone and sandstone reservoirs that lay above them. Shales can be both source rocks and producing reservoirs.

**Spud** - To begin drilling a well. Drilling the very first inch of depth in a well is spudding the well.

**Stripper Well** - A well that produces less than 15 barrels of oil per day.

**Surface Rights** - Mineral rights can be severed from surface rights in a property. The surface rights are all rights in a parcel of land except the mineral interest. Surface rights are servient to the mineral rights. The surface interest enjoys the right to the surface subject to the mineral interest.

**Sweet Crude Oil** - Also known as "sweet crude". Sweet crude oil is crude oil that does not contain significant amounts of hydrogen sulfide ($H_2S$). Sweet crude is preferable to sour crude because it costs less to refine.

**Tank Battery** - A group of tanks in a single location. A tank battery usually includes oil stock tanks and may include a gun barrel and a water tank. Tanker trucks visit tank batteries regularly to load the crude oil that is in the oil stock tanks and haul it to pipeline injection points. Tanker trucks also visit tank batteries regularly to load the water that is stored in the water tanks and haul it away to a disposal well.

**TD** - Total Depth. The maximum depth of a well.

**Tight Formation** - A formation that has relatively low permeability.

**Tool Pusher** - also known simply as the "Pusher". The Tool Pusher is the highest ranking person working for the drilling contractor at a drilling location. A crew of roughnecks is lead by a Driller who controls the hoisting system, rotary system, and pumping system on a drilling rig. Drillers and roughnecks are supervised by the Tool Pusher. Tool Pushers have many years of previous experience as Roughnecks and Drillers.

**Trap** - A natural seal in underground layers of sedimentary rock that prohibits hydrocarbons from migrating vertically through it. When migrating hydrocarbons accumulate under a trap a reservoir is formed.

**Trip** - A trip is the movement of all of the drill pipe or tubing either into or out of a well. "Tripping Out" means pulling all of the drill pipe or tubing out of a well. "Tripping In" means running all of the drill pipe or tubing that is on surface in to a well. Tripping may be performed during drilling operation to change the drill bit if it has become excessively worn. Tripping may be performed during a workover to replace a joint of tubing that has developed a hole in it.

**True Vertical Depth** - Abbreviated as TVD, the true vertical depth of a well or a point in a wellbore as measured from that point directly to the surface along an imaginary vertical line that is perpendicular to the surface and extends through the point, regardless of whether or not the wellbore follows such a perfectly vertical line. The "measured depth" of a well or a point in the well bore, abbreviated as MD, is the depth from the surface as measured along the path of the borehole.

**Tubing** - Small diameter pipe that is lowered in to a cased well that provides a conduit for oil and gas to be produced through. In the United States, tubing is commonly 2-3/8 inches or 2-7/8 inches in diameter.

**Turnkey** - A contractual arrangement where a drilling contractor agrees to drill a well to an agreed total depth with agreed specifications for a fixed price and the Operator is not liable for payment of the fixed price to the drilling contractor unless and until a well is successfully drilled to the agreed total depth and meets the other agreed specifications. A turnkey contract places most of the operational risk of successfully drilling a well on the drilling contractor. If there are unforeseen problems during the drilling operation, the Operator is protected by having a Turnkey contract which limits their drilling cost.

**Undivided Interest** – An ownership interest where a party owns an interest in a property with one or more other parties and their interests are not separated in to separate parcels with separate legal descriptions. Each party owns a percentage of the same property which has only one legal description.

**Viscosity** - A measure of a fluid's resistance to flow. Oilfield units for viscosity are centipoise (cp). A centipoise is one one-hundredth of a poise. A poise is one gram/centimeter/second.

**Volumetric Gas Reservoir** - In a volumetric gas reservoir, gas exists by itself within the pores of the rock without any oil or water at the reservoir boundaries and within a relatively fixed volume. The pressure of the gas simply declines as the gas is produced. Producing a volumetric gas reservoir (also known as a depletion drive gas reservoir) is similar to opening the valve on a scuba diver's air tank and allowing the air to blow out. The most efficient drive mechanism for producing gas is a volumetric reservoir. It provides the highest ultimate recovery.

**Water Drive Gas Reservoir** - In a water drive gas reservoir, there is a large water reservoir below the gas reservoir and it pushes against the gas and displaces the gas like a piston as the gas is produced. If the wellbore perforations are only in the gas zone and completely above the water, the initial production may be at or near 100% gas. Because the water moves up and displaces gas as the gas is produced, the gas reservoir's pressure may not decline significantly. If the permeability is high then the reservoir pressure and the gas flow rate will be nearly constant over time. From the Operator's viewpoint, the well seems as if it will produce at a constant rate indefinitely. This characteristic can make the well appear to be an attractive purchase. However, as soon as the water that is displacing the gas from below reaches the perforations in the wellbore, the gas production will suddenly cease.

Some Operators produce water drive gas reservoirs at very high rates in the hope that they can produce gas from locations in the reservoir that are both above and below the perforations. Others choose to produce these reservoirs at very slow rates so as to minimize the pressure differential between the water and the perforations and thus minimize the odds of "coning" water up to the perforations from the water below. The downside of this method is that any gas that is in the reservoir but above the depth of the perforations will not be produced and will be left in the reservoir at full reservoir pressure. Water drive gas reservoirs have a relatively constant flowing tubing pressure and flow rate until the day when the water reaches the perforations and all gas production suddenly ceases.

**Water Drive Oil Reservoir** - In a water drive oil reservoir, there is a large water reservoir below the oil reservoir and it pushes against the oil and displaces it like a piston. The pressure from the water below acts on the oil and pressurizes it to equal the water's pressure at the oil-water interface. When the wellbore is perforated, the water begins to push the oil toward the wellbore. If the wellbore perforations are only in the oil zone and completely above the water, the initial production may be at or near 100% oil. Over time some of the water will begin to "finger through" inhomogeneities of the oil zone where the relative permeability of water is higher. Eventually some of this water will "break-through" and be seen in the produced fluid along with the oil. From that point forward, the production will include both oil and water. The production rate of oil will decline exponentially over time.

Roughly 80% of all wells have a production decline rate that is between 12% and 30%. A 12% exponential decline rate means that each year a well produces 88% of the amount of oil that it produced in the preceding year. A 30% exponential decline rate means that each year a well produces 70% of the amount of oil that it produced in the preceding year. All other things being equal, an oil reservoir with a water-drive mechanism will have a lower (better) decline rate and a higher ultimate recovery than an equivalent reservoir with any other drive mechanism. Water-drive is the most efficient drive mechanism for producing oil.

**Water-Wet** - A condition where the interfacial tension between the grains of rock in a formation and the formation water is less than the interfacial tension between the grains of the rock and oil in the formation. A water-wet reservoir is preferable to an oil-wet reservoir when initiating a water flood.

**Wet** - A wet formation is a formation with pore space that is 100% saturated with water. Oil and gas cannot be produced from wet zones because wet zones do not contain oil or gas. Porous wet zones containing saline formation water tend to have relatively low resistivity.

**Wildcat** - A well that is drilled far from any previously drilled wells.

**Working Interest** - The Lessee's interest in a petroleum property that is created when an oil and gas lease is executed. The working interest is entitled to all revenues from production after subtracting the mineral interest owner's royalty and any overriding royalty interests that the working interest owner has assigned.

# Oil and Gas Web Sites

State Oil and Gas
Regulatory Agencies

Alabama
http://www.gsa.state.al.us/

California
http://www.conservation.ca.gov/

Colorado
http://cogcc.state.co.us/

Florida
http://www.dep.state.fl.us/water/mines/oil_gas/index.htm

Illinois
http://dnr.state.il.us/mines/dog/

Indiana
http://www.in.gov/dnr/

Kansas
http://www.kcc.state.ks.us/conservation/index.htm

Kentucky
http://oilandgas.ky.gov/

Louisiana
http://dnr.louisiana.gov/min/

Mississippi
http://www.ogb.state.ms.us/

Montana
http://bogc.dnrc.state.mt.us/

Nevada
http://minerals.state.nv.us/

New Mexico
http://www.emnrd.state.nm.us/ocd/

New York
http://www.dec.ny.gov/about/805.html

North Dakota
https://www.dmr.nd.gov/oilgas/

Oklahoma
http://www.occeweb.com/og/oghome.htm

Pennsylvania
http://www.dep.state.pa.us/dep/deputate/minres/oilgas/oilgas.htm

Texas
http://www.rrc.state.tx.us/

Wyoming
http://wogcc.state.wy.us/

## Government

U.S. Energy Information Administration
http://www.eia.doe.gov/

U.S. Energy Information Administration
Annual Energy Outlook
http://www.eia.doe.gov/oiaf/aeo/

U.S. Geological Survey National Oil and Gas Assessment
http://energy.cr.usgs.gov/oilgas/noga/

## Publications

American Oil and Gas Reporter
http://www.aogr.com/

Oil and Gas Investor
http://www.oilandgasinvestor.com/

Rig Zone
http://www.rigzone.com/

# Organizations

American Petroleum Institute
http://www.api.org/

Independent Petroleum Association of America
http://www.ipaa.org/

American Association of Professional Land Men
http://www.ipaa.org/

Society of Petroleum Engineers
http://www.spe.org

American Association of Petroleum Geologists
http://www.aapg.org/

Society of Exploration Geophysicists
http://www.seg.org/

Bureau of Economic Geology
http://www.beg.utexas.edu

# Oil and Gas Prices

CME Futures Contract Quotes
http://www.cmegroup.com/trading/energy/

# Oil and Gas Trade Shows

NAPE - North American Prospect Expo
http://www.napeexpo.com/

PBIOS - Permian Basin International Oil Show
http://www.pbioilshow.org/

# Securities

SEC Reg D Offerings
http://www.sec.gov/answers/regd.htm

Securities and Exchange Commission Oil and Gas Scams Page
http://www.sec.gov/investor/pubs/oilgasscams.htm

# Public

Bureau of Economic Geology
http://www.beg.utexas.edu

North Dakota Oil and Gas Leasing Considerations
https://www.dmr.nd.gov/oilgas/leasingconsiderations.pdf

ExxonMobil Energy Outlook to 2030
http://www.exxonmobil.com/corporate/files/news_pub_eo_2009.pdf

Weiss Energy Hall at the Houston Museum of Natural Science
http://www.hmns.org

Permian Basin Petroleum Museum
http://www.petroleummuseum.org/

# About the Author

Mike May is a Licensed Professional Petroleum Engineer. He has over 20 years of experience in the oil and gas industry. His geographic experience includes oil and gas wells located in Texas, Louisiana, California, North Dakota, Washington, Wyoming, the Gulf of Mexico, Trinidad, Argentina, the United Kingdom, Romania, Azerbaijan, North Africa, Iraq, India, Vietnam, and Malaysia.

He has advised ExxonMobil, Shell, Apache, Conoco, Statoil Hydro, Newfield Exploration, Nexen Petroleum, Cairn Energy, Reliance Industries of India, and more than 50 smaller independent oil companies.

Mike has spoken to oil and gas industry audiences around the world from oil companies in Houston to the Geological Society of London to technology seminars in India. He has spoke about a wide range of advanced downhole technologies including formation fluid sampling and pressure testing.

Mike specializes in formation evaluation and while representing one of the big three service companies he was responsible for all electric wireline operations for a major international oil company with operations in 15 countries. Prior to that he performed over 700 open hole logging jobs in the field, analyzed thousands of formations, and helped clients assess the commercial viability of hundreds of wells by analyzing open hole logs at the casing point.

Mike is an expert in the computer modeling of downhole perforation performance. He has designed numerous perforating jobs from Texas to Iraq.

He has been the lead negotiator of several oilfield service contracts with a total value in nine figures.

Mike has experience in Petrophysics, Log Analysis, Downhole Formation Fluid Testing and Sampling, Electric Wireline Operations, Petroleum Geology, Reservoir Engineering, Drilling, Completions, Seismic and Geophysics.

Mike lives in Houston, Texas.
He is the owner of Limestone Oil.
Mike creates oil and gas investment packages in the United States.

Mike May, P.E.
(832) 382-9976
mike.may @ investing in oil and gas.com
www. investing in oil and gas .com

Also visit www.limestoneoil.com.

Coming Soon:

# The Oil and Gas Investor's Check List:

**A Step-By-Step Method for
Investors to Evaluate
Oil and Gas Well
Drilling and Workover
Investment Opportunities
and
Decide Whether or Not to Invest**

17145699R00292

Made in the USA
Lexington, KY
29 August 2012